# WE NEED EACH OTHER

# WE NEED EACH OTHER

## *The Miracle of Relationships*

HOW TO
BUILD THEM

♦

HOW TO
MEND THEM

♦

HOW TO
KEEP THEM

## KEITH & GLADYS HUNT

Zondervan Books
Zondervan Publishing House
Grand Rapids, Michigan

Previously published as *Not Alone: The Necessity of Relationships*

Zondervan Books are published by the Zondervan Publishing House
1415 Lake Drive, S.E., Grand Rapids, Michigan 49506

**Library of Congress Cataloging-in-Publication Data**

Hunt, Keith.
 [Not alone]
 We need each other : the necessity of relationships / Keith and
Gladys Hunt.
 p. cm.
 Reprint. Originally published: Not alone. Grand Rapids : Zondervan
Books, 1985.
 Includes biographical references.
 ISBN 0-310-26401-4
 1. Interpersonal relations—Religious aspects—Christianity.
 2. Christian life—1960– I. Hunt, Gladys M. II. Title.
BV4597.52.H85 1990
248.4—dc20                                        89–39914
                                                        CIP

All Scripture quotations, unless otherwise noted, are taken from the *Holy Bible: New International Version* (North American Edition). Copyright © 1973, 1978, 1984 by the International Bible Society. Used by permission of Zondervan Bible Publishers.

*Edited by John D. Sloan*
*Designed by Kim Koning*

*Printed in the United States of America*

90  91  92  93  94  95 / PP / 10  9  8  7  6  5  4  3

*To our friends,*
*many of whom are also family*

# Contents

# Preface

C. S. Lewis called it "the intolerable compliment"—this awesome offer of a relationship with God. Our first instinct is to hide from so terrible a friendship; yet when we accept, we find, to our astonishment, that we were made for this—to relate to the living God.

It would be hard to miss how much God wants to relate to us. He came in the flesh—

> Our God contracted to a span,
> Incomprehensibly made man,

—to rescue us. He did it all, everything that needed doing, to make our relating possible. He not only *came* all the way, but he endured the rebuke of men, the agony of the cross, and the disjuncture of death. And his final triumph meant that the way was open for us to know the living God.

The more we look at it, the more obvious it becomes that the world exists so that God may love us. We were made to relate to him, and therefore our highest activity is to respond to his invitation.

As we draw closer to this Christ who came for us, we see him loving God and loving people. He tells us to love one another and to love our neighbor as ourself. Something else now becomes clearer: we have suspected all along that we were also *made for this*—to relate lovingly to each other as creatures of God.

We hang our heads in shame because we thought we had to do something big for God, like building an organization, saying fine words, or impressing the world. Instead, God wants us to have the deep satisfaction of knowing and loving him—and each other. How could we have missed such obvious truth? He is concerned about our relationships, even though building them is often the thing we do least well.

*      *      *

We have been talking about relationships with students and families for over twenty years. Although we are not experts, we know that this is what life is for: to love God and to love each other.

In one sense we have been writing this book all our lives, because relationships are to be lived, not just talked about. Sometimes we get discouraged with our progress and say to ourselves, "You've lived this long, and you're still working on that?" At other times we feel God's Spirit flooding us with his kind of love and sense the overflow reaching out to build others. We are still in process—learning how to love God more fully; learning how to love each other more perfectly; learning how to be the son or daughter, parent, grandparent, friend, brother, or sister God wants us to be.

It is scary to see what is happening in the world. People use each other instead of loving each other, as if a strange myopia, a self-absorption, were causing them to shut out others' needs and feelings, and to say, "I gotta get mine while I can."

It is a frightening, uncaring scene: people fearing the risk of being known, moving farther away instead of closer; people rushing through each other's lives to grab some fleeting happiness on their way to somewhere else; people seeking pleasure instead of keeping promises; people touching only each other's skins, never the heart; people unconcerned about the hungry, the lost, the lonely.

Such self-centered ways deny what it means to be human. We were made for more than we know.

This book is about being related to each other by God's grace, and it is based on the Christian heritage our families gave us, the heritage we spend our lives passing on to others.

There are no *ordinary* people. You have never talked to a mere mortal. Nations, cultures, arts, civilisations—these are mortal, and their life is to ours as the life of a gnat. But it is immortals whom we joke with, work with, marry, snub, and exploit—immortal horrors or everlasting splendours. This does not mean that we are to be perpetually solemn. We must play. But our merriment must be of that kind (and it is, in fact, the merriest kind) that exists between people who have, from the outset, taken each other seriously—no flippancy, no superiority, no presumption. And our charity must be a real and costly love, with deep feeling for the sins in spite of which we love the sinner—no mere tolerance, or indulgence that parodies love as flippancy parodies merriment. . . . (Because we are made in the image of God) it is with the awe and the circumspection proper to them, that we should conduct all our dealings with one another, all friendships, all loves, all play, all politics. There are no *ordinary* people.

C. S. Lewis
*The Weight of Glory*

*chapter* 1

# Made in an Image, Marred in a Relationship

We were made for each other. Life has little meaning apart from this fact. Autonomous man is a myth. Ask people who are fully alive what gives life meaning, and they will tell you about their relationships.

We were made to relate to God and to each other. God made us *relational beings*, which is what being human is all about. Yet this has become our complicated problem: we know how to split the atom, how to get to the moon, and how to make robots do our bidding, but in our relationships we often experience only disappointment and failure. They are the most difficult part of our lives. If relationships threaten our sense of well-being, we often turn away and make people our lowest priority.

People living together and never touching each other's lives. Lonely people hiding in separate apartments on the same floor, afraid to reach out and share their lives. Haunted people filling their world with noise, shutting out people with exploding decibels of sounds. People never feeling known or loved. No one ought to have to cry alone or die alone or feel alone in a world where all share the same vulnerabilities and frailties of being human. We were made for each other, for relationships.

To understand how important this is we must return to our beginnings to see how God made people and what he had in mind when he created us.

### Back to the Beginning

A grand cadence, a stirring rhythm marks the unfolding of the creative work of God in Genesis 1. God *speaks* a world into being, creating all things by the word of his power. Six times this pattern repeats:

And God said, Let there be . . . and it was so.

The Creator creates and furnishes a universe by his commands. No wonder the morning stars sang together and all the angels shout for joy (Job 38:7).

And God saw it was good.

The pattern changes at this point in creation. God is about to do something new:

*Then* God said, "Let *us* make man in *our* image,
in our likeness. . . ."
So God created man in his own image,
in the image of God he created him;
male and female he created them.

(Genesis 1:26, 27, italics ours)

With an economy of words our beginning is explained. Unlike prior creation, God does not speak mankind into existence—he does not say, "Let there be man." Rather, he says, "let us make man . . ." and then he scoops up the dust of the earth, forms a man and breathes into his nostrils the breath of life (Genesis 2:7). A mysterious synthesis: the dust of the earth and the life of God, the material and the spiritual. God does not first make a soul and wrap a body around it like a watchmaker who first drafts the inner works and then inserts it in a case.[1] No. God makes a complete being: spirit, soul (mind), and body.[2]

Emil Brunner comments: "Man, in contrast from all the rest of creation, has not merely been created by and through God, but in and for God. . . . Hence he can and should understand himself in God alone."[3]

Two powerful truths emerge from this brief Genesis creation account. First, people are made in the image of God, in his likeness. But in what ways are we made in his likeness? Does his image have anything to do with our ability to relate? Such an investigation will lead us to a greater understanding of ourselves and God.

Second, the image of God comprises both male and female. The *man* of Genesis 1 is the word that describes generic mankind. *Today's English Version* reads, "So God created human beings, making them to be like himself. He created them male and female." The image of God is a dual modality.

## Made in the Image of God

What does it mean to be made in the image of God? The idea is overwhelming. We want to shout, "Who, me?" John Ruskin said that our lapses in quality living come from forgetting who we are. We need to be reminded. Man is the crown of all creation! David expressed his awe in Psalm 8 when he exclaimed:

> What is man that thou art mindful of him,
>   and the son of man that thou dost care for him?
> Yet thou hast made him a little less than God,[4]
>   and dost crown him with glory and honor.
> Thou hast given him dominion over the works of
>     thy hands;
>   thou hast put all things under his feet.
>
> (Psalm 8:4–6, RSV)

"It is the image of God in man that marks man as God's peculiar possession, uniquely sacred as is no other created being, and in consequence of which man is fitted to fulfill holy purposes," writes Dwight Small.[5] He contends that the image of God is not descriptive of man's essential being *in and of himself*; the image of God describes a living, dynamic relationship between God and man. Whatever man is, he is in relation to God. He is like God but less than God.

But hasn't the Fall obliterated the image of God in man? The phrase "image of God" is used in three Old Testament passages. The first, Genesis 1:26–27, has already been given. The second passage is Genesis 5:1–2: "When God created man, he made him in the likeness of God. He created them male and female and blessed them. And when they were created, he called them 'man.'" This is basically a summary of Genesis 1. The third use of that phrase is in Genesis 9:6 when, after the flood, God decrees the value of human life: "Whoever sheds the blood of man, by man shall his blood be shed; for in the image of God has God made man." The image of God is still present in man, though it is marred by sin. Nowhere does Scripture say that the image of God in man has been destroyed.

In what way do human beings bear the image of God? Obviously we are not omniscient, omnipresent, and omnipotent. These *omni* words, which signify God's power, infinitude, and perfection, blind our eyes to the wonder of being created in God's image.

### We were made rational beings

Human beings, made in God's image, have the capacity to think, to reason. God himself is all intelligence; our intelligence is grounded in his. He made us word-partners with himself so we can communicate together. The use of language is a rational process. He has given us shining symbols, known as words, that allow us to talk with him and with each other, to express ideas, feelings, to define ourselves.

We can communicate concepts; we can define goals and order our priorities to achieve them; we can think abstract thoughts and contemplate God and our own nature (as we are doing in this book); and we can create because we are related to the ultimate Creator. Remember that the next time originality bursts upon you.

### We were made moral beings

God has made us responsible people. We can choose. The volitional aspect of our nature mirrors the dignity God bestowed on us when he made us. God is the standard for all truth; he establishes morality. God has written truth on our hearts (Romans 2:15) and gives to us the gift of choice. It is a terrifying thing to realize that we may say *yes* or *no* to God and that our decision can be binding for eternity. Our choices affect not only our relationship to God, however, but our relationships to all members of the community of which we are a part. Because we are made relational beings, there is no such thing as a private choice.

## We were made spiritual beings

We are physical, tied to the earth; we are spiritual, tied to heaven. We contemplate our being and ask "Who am I?" We feel intuitively that we are more than body. We are spiritual persons, and our greatest longings lie in this part of our being. We can look at ourselves objectively, evaluate, and even judge ourselves as spiritual beings.

If we are honest we know what we are. We are not autonomous, but dependent, and eternity is written on our hearts. We struggle toward something infinite, something lasting, and it is this that drives us toward a relationship with God, although not all would be willing to admit it. But we have within us the ability to respond to God and to be God's friend as Abraham was.

## We were made relational beings

Dietrich Bonhoeffer, writing on Genesis 1–3, says that man is the image of God, not in spite of but because of his *bodiliness*. "For in his bodiliness he is related to other bodies, he is there for others."[6] Just as God is there for others, so man who images God must be for others.

Even our sexuality—God's design that urges males and females toward each other—profoundly verifies our relational nature. The man is whole in himself, and the woman is whole in herself, but each is only whole in communion with the other, for no one knows himself in isolation but always in fellowship. Interaction with a counterpart of humanity helps us define who we are. It is not the sex act we are talking about, but sexuality—a way of "being" in the image of God.

Personal communion is what the image of God is about. Lewis Smedes insists that "biblical revelation tells us to stop thinking of ourselves as isolated islands of rational God-likeness and think of ourselves instead as coming into real humanity when we live in genuine personal fellowship with others."[7]

Because we are relational by God's design, we have an inner longing to share our emotions and to be known. We have feelings and reactions to our world and to each other. God has emotions. He responds to his creatures and his creation. He has compassion and sorrow. He reveals himself. We have an inborn desire to do the same, to experience intimacy with another human being. We know love because he himself is love and has loved us. We communicate, we understand, we empathize.

We can transcend ourselves because we are in his image. You can tell me something from your life that is not part of my experience, and I can reach out of my own smallness and feel what you feel and share in your experience. To transcend myself simply means to go beyond my knowledge or limits. God is ultimately transcendent, but he has given us a portion of it when he made us in his image.

God is relational in his very being. A community exists within the Godhead. From the beginning God speaks of himself in the plural. "Let us make man in our image . . ." (Genesis 1:26). Consistently in the pages of Scripture, a picture unfolds of a God who exists in three Persons—the Trinity. Clearly the members of the Godhead have a relationship with each other. What can we learn from the model of our God-in-community, since we are made relational beings in his image? What can be said about the harmony, the unity of purpose, the affirmation of distinctive Persons within the Godhead that might instruct us in our relationships with others? God and man have this in common: They are beings in relationship.

Discussing the image of God reminds us of who we are and gives us a sense of awe about our being. Look in the mirror tomorrow morning and remind yourself, "You were made in the image of God." This simple exercise has the potential of changing your view of self, your expectations for yourself, your fellowship with God, and your regard for others who are also made in his image.

## Male and Female in the Image of God

It seems strange that people still need to be reminded of this fact: that the image of God is both female and male—one humanity in two distinct persons. Genesis 1:27 makes that very clear. God gave his blessing to the man and the woman, putting the earth and its creatures in their care. Then he evaluated the culmination of his creation as *very good*.

Genesis 2 tells the creation story in more detail. In this account the male was created first and tended the garden alone. God made a clear statement about Adam's aloneness: It was not good. It was his first negative evaluation about his creation. God gave the man a show-and-tell demonstration that left no doubt about the loneliness of this first Walden Pond experience. God underscored the fact that *aloneness* is not part of his plan.

Adam was assigned the task of naming the beasts of the field and the birds of the air. What a marvelous way to view this fresh creation—from kangaroos to giraffes to hoopoe birds! But the longer Adam looked, the lonelier he became. There was no one like him. He looked over all of creation and faced his own uniqueness. But God, who knows the joy of fellowship within himself, remedied Adam's plight. He took a part of Adam and made someone like him, yet different, and brought her to the man. A woman. Adam shouted with delight in recognition of his own counterpart:

"This is now bone of my bones
and flesh of my flesh."

At that moment Adam fulfilled the one part God gave him to play in the drama of his own creation.[8] He did not know what he lacked or what to look for. God provided, and Adam affirmed God's provision.

The details of creation are brief, but profound in their implications. God fashioned the woman by removing a rib from the man. Her origin was not the same as that of the man. She is related to him in a significant way. She is unique in creation, unmistakably her own person. Yet she was taken out of man. And the man surrendered part of himself to the making of the woman. He cannot separate himself from her, and neither can she isolate herself from him, for they are interdependent. It is God's doing, a mystery.[9]

When God saw the man alone, why didn't he make another male? The triune God again is the model: the Persons are alike in kind, yet different. Could it be that something about God is best mirrored by a woman and that another aspect of his person is best imaged by a man? If this is so, and we believe it to be one explanation for the existence of two sexes, then our relational responsibilities in the human community are clear. We need each other in all our enterprises, not just in the marriage relationship. Men and women are partners in experiencing what it means to be human. They complement each other's expression of person-hood. Although it remains a paradox, it is a delightful one: so much alike, yet not alike; different from each other, yet the same.

God had more in mind than the general human enterprise, however, when he created man and woman. Adam's delight at finding a perfect counterpart and their subsequent union in marital partnership is God's completion of humanity. They were one flesh, modeling the unity within the Godhead. This husband-wife unity is the prototype for all other human relationships. God called them Adam (mankind)—Mr. and Mrs. Adam, made in the image of God, and together, naked and unashamed, they tended the Garden of Eden, knowing each other and God, and accepting one another.

Barth writes movingly about this first pair: "In this divinely ordained relationship they ... had no cause for mutual reproach. They had no need to envy their respective advan-tages. . . . Nor had they anything to conceal from each other. They were together without embarrassment or disquiet. They were not against one another but with one another, the man being the husband to the woman, and the woman the wife to the man."[10]

What incredible beginnings we have: This ineffable Creator God, full of love, stoops down to make human beings—male and female—in his image so they can enjoy each other. Then God walks and talks with them, letting himself be known!

## Marred Relationships

No record tells us how long Adam and his wife Eve lived in such bliss together. Undoubtedly it was a life of both quantity and quality, fresh in the dew of God's creation. But the question of how long is not as important to us as that it *was*. The relationship of that first man and woman to God and to each other creates within all of us what C. S. Lewis called *an inconsolable longing* now that we live on this side of what is so aptly called the Fall.

The scenario of the Fall has been replayed over and over again in the lives of people who, like the woman of Genesis 3, are caught off guard by temptation. The scheme is a specialty with the evil one, and it works so well that he hasn't bothered to change his tactics to this day. It is the art of temptation.

If God creates a being in his own image, then he must create a person with freedom. Only a free person can worship God and do his will[11]—otherwise the being is a robot lacking choice. Inherent in freedom is the idea of having options, even the option to do wrong. Yet because he is creature and not Creator, a person has boundaries to his freedom. Boundaries remind him from whom he received his freedom. He is finite, not infinite. He is creature, not Creator. Herein lies temptation's opportunities.

God gave the man and the woman the world to enjoy, a garden to tend, full of good things, but he set one boundary: "You must not eat fruit from the tree that is in the middle of the garden. . . ." This boundary, the only limitation God gave—this tree—became the focal point of temptation.

The Tempter is a wily serpent and exceedingly clever. His approach to Eve is thoroughly pious. In his crafty way he gets the woman to discuss God's character, and by dangling an exaggeration before her and drawing her into a debate on his terms, he began to sow seeds of doubt in her mind about God's goodness.

Thus, the serpent struck two blows to Eve's sense of well-being. First, he suggested that she took God too seriously

(Genesis 3:1–4), and second, he made her distrustful of God's goodness (Genesis 3:5). At this point the conversation ended, and he waited for the venom of his words to take effect. Had he poisoned Eve's resolve?

The force of the words of Scripture is that she meditated on the fruit of the tree (Genesis 3:6). The more she focused on it, the better it looked, and besides, the fruit had a secret potential for self-expansion. Her senses pressured her. She reached out and took the fruit. *To be like God* . . .

Eve ate and "gave some to her husband, who was with her, and he ate it." No sinner wants to be alone in sin. And so the history of mankind's fall from grace began with something very small and quiet, but the event has an ever-widening effect. So simple an act; so hard to undo. God will taste poverty and death before *"take and eat"* become verbs of salvation.[12]

"Then the eyes of both of them were opened, and they realized they were naked; so they sewed fig leaves together and made coverings for themselves" (Genesis 3:7). They were ashamed. Before they had been naked and not ashamed. Suddenly nakedness was not appropriate. They wanted to hide themselves. Shame is an appropriate response. In that sense, shame is good. Today some are bent on expunging all shame from our experience, as if it were possible to return to Eden. It is not that nakedness is wrong; it is a statement that modesty befits a fallen world.

Lewis Smedes describes shame as the "painful feeling that we are not the persons we ought to be: to be ashamed is to have a sense of our fractured lives, a longing to be whole. . . . It is closely linked with sexuality because sexuality is deeply woven into the texture of our very beings. . . . [In paradise] a man and a woman played and worked together as persons whose lives were totally integrated into their entire life. They looked at each other and each saw a person in whom he/she was wholly involved as a helper fit for the other. They had no shame because they had no sense of being anything but what they ought to be: body-persons in loving partnership. . . . When Adam and Eve first sensed that their partnership was marred, they became aware of each other as bodies separate from persons. And so the sense of shame came in."[13]

Dwight Small comments that the very first consequence of the Fall had to do with the man-woman relationship and not with God's response to their sin. What was supposed to be so self-enhancing destroyed their togetherness.

The Lord God walked in the garden in the cool of the day and called out, "Where are you?" At the sound of his voice the man and his wife, pathetically clothed in their fig leaves, hid themselves from the presence of God (Genesis 3:8–9). Having known the Creator's fellowship and the fullness of life in relationship to him, they now cowered in fear. And it has been this way ever since. In spite of their outward show of bravado about sin, sinners do not like the presence of Righteousness.

The bad news is their guilt before God that makes them hide; the good news is his calling them and finding them. "Where are you?" Do you think he didn't know? His words have the mark of grace in them. He wanted them to know where they were in relation to himself. Adam answers, "I heard you in the garden, and I was afraid because I was naked; so I hid." God's response is only to ask questions. "Who told you that you were naked? Have you eaten from the tree . . . ?" (Genesis 3:8–11).

Here begins the game that has become classic among mankind—passing the blame. Adam could have confessed his stupidity and error; instead, he indirectly blames God and more overtly blames the woman. In doing so, he also denies his likeness to God: his moral nature, his responsibility for choice. He says, "The woman *you* put here with me—she gave me some fruit from the tree and I ate it." When God turns to the woman, she blames the serpent for deceiving her. "Dear God, it was the serpent *you* put in this garden" (Genesis 3:12–14, paraphrase).

In the end they wanted to make God the culprit; they refused to take responsibility for themselves. God was in the dock, with man the chief witness against him.

Life for both the man and the woman changed drastically. The disorder of sin affected their bodies and their world. For the woman it was pain in childbirth and a prediction that her relationship to her husband would change: "Your desire will be for your husband, and he will rule over you" (Genesis 3:16). Trouble came into the world that man still had to tend, now through painful toil, thorns, thistles; by the sweat of his brow would he work until he returned to dust (Genesis 3:17–19).

Before this time Adam and Eve had known only life. Death had never crossed their path; they had no experience with it. What was it? Someone may look at this account in Genesis and say that the serpent was right, that Adam and Eve did not drop dead. But there is more to death than this. They did die spiritually. They had broken their relationship with God.

## Broken Relationships

Can you imagine Adam's and Eve's sorrow over the loss in their own relationship? The perfection of harmony, transparency, and utter ease within their union is suddenly shattered. Dwight Small expresses it this way: "The woman who was given to complete the man now exists as his contradiction;

she is with him, yet in a new and threatening way she is his rival. . . . In sinning against God, becoming independent of Him and breaking the covenant, they discovered that their integrity toward one another was altered."[14]

Originally Adam had named his counterpart *woman*, because she was taken out of man (Genesis 2:23). This name had declared his identification with her. She had been part of him. Now he changed her name to E*ve*, because she is the mother of all people (Genesis 3:20). This change of name indicates, perhaps subtly, a demotion: "No longer does she stand alongside him in equality, sharing Adam's full personhood; rather, she represents a means whereby certain ends will be achieved. Adam now looks upon her instrumentally, defining her not in terms of *being* but of *doing*. She is no longer *person* but *performer*. She is *means*, not end, *supplement*, not complement, *inferior*, not equal. Here is the essence of the struggle that reaches down to our own time and the women's liberation movement."[15] God's prediction in Genesis 3:16— "He shall rule over you"—became even more devastatingly clear when Lamech took two wives (Genesis 4:19). He completely broke away from the model of the one-flesh concept of Genesis 2:24.

What about their relationship to God? Suddenly access to God was changed. Sin separates. God no longer walked and talked with them in a fellowship of joy and purity. A flaming sword barred them from Eden. In Genesis 4 the establishment of a sacrificial system demonstrates God's more distant contact with them, yet God's marvelous grace bridges the sin barrier; it is the story of human history. He does not reject Adam and Eve and blot them out forever, but he relates to them now on a different basis.

A distortion of all good things results from mankind's disobedience. Work is distorted. A twisting of meanings scars the lives of human beings. Disintegration of values saps the world's system. There are still many flaming swords in the world today, keeping us away from Edenic perfection.

Not only our relationship with God has been affected by the Fall, but our relationships with others. The pain of our shame disorients us, distances us from God and from other people. We who were made for these relationships find them our nemesis.

"The past in its pastness is not what concerns me but the past as something present. . . . I am delving into Adam to unriddle him and myself," wrote Gerhard Nebel. And that is what we have been doing. The question now is, How do we live in a fallen world? To what extent can our relationships be restored?

---

¹Lewis Smedes, *Sex for Christians* (Grand Rapids: Wm. B. Eerdmans Publishing Company, 1976), 28.

²The tragedy of man's sin is evidenced in the brokenness of our original wholeness. Man is cut off from God spiritually; he becomes vain in his imaginations; and his body is subject to death and decay. The good news of the gospel is that God brings us back to himself, makes us alive in areas where we were dead, and will even rescue our bodies on the day of resurrection. Believers will not be disembodied spirits in heaven, but will have new bodies.

³Emil Brunner, *Man in Revolt* (Philadelphia: Westminster Press, 1947), 92.

⁴The King James Version translates this phrase as "a little lower than the angels" and the New International Version renders it "a little lower than the heavenly beings." The

translators, perhaps, are showing their reticence to have anyone misunderstand, but the Hebrew word is *Elohim*, meaning God. The Revised Standard Version comes closest to the original in rendering it "a little less than God."

[5] Dwight Small, *Christian: Celebrate Your Sexuality* (Old Tappan, N.J.: Fleming H. Revell Co., 1974), 105.

[6] Dietrich Bonhoeffer, *Creation and Fall: A Theological Interpretation of Genesis 1–3* (London: SCM Press Ltd., 1959), 33.

[7] Smedes, *Sex for Christians*, 33.

[8] Small, *Christian: Celebrate Your Sexuality*, 136.

[9] We are indebted to Dwight Small for his stimulating book, *Christian: Celebrate Your Sexuality*, and we commend it to our readers.

[10] Karl Barth, *Church Dogmatics* III (Edinburgh: T. & T. Clark, 1960), 4:150.

[11] Small, *Christian: Celebrate Your Sexuality*, 154.

[12] Derek Kidner, *Genesis, An Introduction and Commentary* (London: Tyndale Press, 1967), 68.

[13] Smedes, *Sex for Christians*, 47–48.

[14] Small, *Christian: Celebrate Your Sexuality*, 158, 163.

[15] Ibid., 161.

*chapter* 2

# Rescue from a Troubled Land

The small seed of self-contradiction that Adam and Eve planted in the Garden of Eden has borne bitter fruit in human life. From their loins has come a people often in flight from God, from themselves, and from their relationships.

In the tragic story of Cain, the first-born of Adam and Eve, the terrible truth about sin—what it does to people and their relationships—shocks us all. The tale is tersely told in Genesis 4, but what is told emphasizes the depth of Cain's crime and his arrogance before God.

When he came before God at the altar with his gift, Cain's heart was full of Cain, not God. He had his own idea of what should have pleased the Creator, and when his offering was disqualified and his brother Abel's offering accepted, his response was anger instead of penitence.

Cain, consumed with jealousy, invited his brother Abel to go into the field with him. Because he was accustomed to being first and angry at having his offering rejected, Cain got rid of his rival. He killed Abel. He no longer saw Abel as a person made in the image of God or as a brother; Abel was an obstacle.

God came again with questions: "Where is your brother Abel?" It was reminiscent of his query to Adam and Eve. Cain's callous response revealed his heart: "Am I my brother's keeper?" God did not make him his brother's *keeper*, but his brother's *brother*.

## The Land of Nod

Now Cain lost everything. The soil had drunk his brother's blood. Not only the thorns and thistles, but his blood cried out in accusation.[1] Cain was afraid, full of anxiety because he would be a wanderer on the earth, and he imagined all sorts of evil against himself. The earth was no longer a safe place for Cain. He went to dwell in the land of Nod, which means *wandering* and *restlessness*. He became the prototype of insecure mankind.

Derek Kidner remarks that God's concern for the innocent (Abel) is matched only by his care for the sinner.[2] God gave Cain a mark, not a stigma but a safe-conduct pass, so that the near kinsmen of Abel would not take vengeance into their own hands. In doing this, God made himself Cain's protector and grace once more overflowed in the affairs of men. The words of the text are solemn, however: "So Cain went out from the LORD's presence."

Unrepentant Cain wanted God's protection, but not his

presence. He set out to make some success of his independence; he wanted to establish a self-sufficient society, a
society without regard to God, a society that the New
Testament calls "the world." His was the first secular
enterprise. He built a city; his descendants were skilled in
arts and crafts and masters of iron works and tools (Genesis
4:17–24). Made in the image of God, Cain and his descendants began to subdue the earth.

The seeds of sorrow are everywhere in this story: Lamech
tried to improve on God's marriage plan by taking two wives;
tools and iron works were fashioned into weapons; Lamech
exulted in his murder of a youth. Cain's family was a
microcosm, and its pattern of technical prowess and moral
failure is that of humanity.[3]

Helmut Thielicke comments that the Cainite strain exists
in all the great civilizations of history.[4] Temples, pyramids,
glorious cathedrals, discoveries, inventions, symphonies,
sculptures, and tapestries—there are all kinds of cultural
riches that do not acknowledge the Creator who provides the
very elements we use in our work and pleasure. And if we
look closely, it becomes obvious that the finest and best of
men's works are tainted by love of power, bloodshed,
selfishness, destruction, abuse of others, and personal
anguish. Is there not in every art the cry for redemption from
the land of Nod? asks Thielicke. Living in this kind of world,
we, too, long for redemption from the land of Nod, from
anxiety over self, and from wandering and restlessness.

## The Origins of Self-Esteem

We were born into a world that is complicated by the
confusion of sin. We were made in the image of God to relate
to him and to each other. But it is easy to forget who we are
and that we have this link with the Creator.

Our earliest encounters with our own corner of this world leave an imprint on us. So many factors make up our heritage—genes, chromosomes, grandparents, uncles and aunts, and of course, our parents. We come equipped with certain physical, emotional, and intellectual characteristics, and we have handicaps and sensitivities we did not choose. We bear a family likeness, yet we are different. We have all the potential inherent in being human, of being unique selves.

The way we are treated in the early years of life profoundly affects our view of our self. Some would say that even unborn children are affected by the mother's joy or dismay at the pregnancy. Happy parents give off happy vibrations. You have a head start if you grow up with parents who think their children are the nicest thing that has happened to the world. Babies hear approval in the voice, see approval on the face of those who care for them. When a two-year-old wakes up from a nap, he is cuddled and kissed; his mother sings to him as she ties his shoes. This child knows he is loved and in turn feels that the world is really quite a nice place. Another small child is left to call and cry at length after waking, and he is greeted with annoyance that his nap was so brief. This child feels he is bothersome and frets about his world. He doesn't feel safe. Such small things in our fallen world—yet these form our self-esteem.

When you bring your report card home to your parents— you have four A's and one B—you are pleased you have done so well. But then your father says, "Let's see if we can bring that B up to an A." No comment on four A's. However well you do, it is never good enough.

You spill the milk as you pour it into your glass and make a mess. Your mother says, "Oh, you! . . . If there's a wrong way to do something, you'll find it." If she says that once, it doesn't matter, but if this response becomes a pattern, you begin to feel wrong about yourself. The mother of one of our friends used to comment in a joking way when introducing her to acquaintances: "Yes, this is my ugly duckling." Although our friend was loved, she grew up feeling ugly.

All humans need positive self-concept feelings if they are to flourish. Fathers and mothers need them, and so do grandparents, small boys and girls, and middle-size ones, too. These feelings include *belonging, worth, competence, virtue,* and *power.*[5] Individuals possess these in varying degrees, but they are the basic building blocks of self-esteem. Those who study human behavior believe that people with high, medium, and low self-esteem live in markedly different worlds. If that is so, what can we learn from exploring these self-concept feelings, not just for ourselves, but for others in our life?

A sense of belonging means "I am wanted, I belong here, I am safe here." That sentence plucks a respondent chord in everyone's heart. Belonging is crucial. God has placed us in families, given us a people to whom we belong, and when we are born the second time—our spiritual rebirth—we are put in another family—the church. Our need to belong is inherent; we were made relational beings.

A sense of worth says, "I count for something. I have value. I respect myself." Permitting domination by another is the result of lacking a sense of worth. Drugs, sexual promiscuity, physical abuse (battered children or battered wife syndrome), and other, less dramatic failures come from the want of this self-esteem.

A sense of competence says, "I can do it." The Horatio Alger tales of success and stories like *The Little Engine That Could* are popular because they are based on the belief that a sense of competence is worth inspiring. It is almost the hallmark of the American way of life to believe that someone born in a log cabin can become president. A proper sense of competence, however, does not overrate itself or trample others, but rather, it is simply an inner sense of adequacy that enables a person to find his place in life. Therefore, this competence hinges on a sense of belonging and worth.

A sense of virtue says, "I know what is right; a moral and ethical standard gives boundaries to my life." In a permissive society this self-concept feeling has been neglected. Since life offers too many choices, and since it offers them without a standard by which to measure value, we are adrift in a turbulent sea of ideas. This self-concept feeling is a plumb line for life and encourages a feeling of security. The lack of moral standards in contemporary society has created a vacuum in individual lives in which cults with strong rules and prohibitions have flourished. People are looking for the discipline of a standard, and they suffer great insecurity without it.

A sense of power—"I can change things; I can influence situations and people,"—is a valid self-concept feeling. It is closely related to a feeling of significance and worth. To understand how important this is to self-esteem we need only think of the self-concept of the truly *powerless*, who can make no difference and who control nothing.

Each of these basic self-concept feelings are important enough to be counterfeited. When they are lacking in a life, ugly evidences of counterfeits appear—self-importance, bragging, possessiveness, self-righteousness, and bullying.

When we feel wobbly on any of these points, the Tempter is quick to exploit us. He accuses us; he tells us lies. The Apostle Paul once wrote that "we are not unaware of his schemes" (2 Corinthians 2:11), but he is wiser than most of us. We repeat Satan's lies when we call ourselves names. "I'm so stupid, ugly, hopeless." Why listen to him, instead of God? We reject the very compliments that would affirm us. "Oh, anybody could have done that." Or "You can't see all the mistakes in it." Or if we are pious we say things like, "It wasn't me, it was the Lord." We become unbelievers about our value, forgetting every truth we have known about ourselves. We manufacture counterfeit self-esteem, which gets us into more trouble.

It is a bad disease, this low self-esteem. It keeps us from the very relationships that would heal us, and it twists our humanity out of shape. *Self* becomes a cult, absorbing all our energy. We were made for relationships, not for this endless fussing over who we are.

## Defending Our Weakness

The struggle against the *dis*ease within us takes peculiar shapes. We want to hide our weaknesses and our inferiorities, and hiding them only makes relationships more difficult. We try to defend ourselves against the anxiety we feel.

In speaking to university students on this subject, we have illustrated it this way:

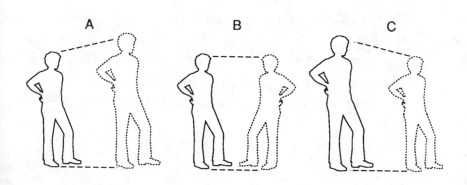

Persons A, B, and C are all the same size. Person A, feeling insecure about himself, projects himself larger than life and plays a game of one-upmanship with everybody. If you have just bought a backpack, he has backpacked all over the country. He loves to talk about *his* exploits, not yours.

Person B presents himself as he is. He is an up-front person. What he is inside, he is outside. He has nothing to prove. He's not perfect, maybe, but he knows what he is.

Person C projects himself smaller than life. He always has a need, a problem, an inadequacy. He presents an image of weakness. He can't do it. He has found this a good way to get attention and get out of responsibility.

This is obviously an oversimplification of the complexity of personhood, but it illustrates the truth about defense mechanisms and lack of self-esteem. For example, answer these questions about A, B, and C.

Which person would walk into a room and expect to be disliked?

Which person would expect to dislike everyone in the room? Why?

What do these two have in common?

Which person would find it difficult to have a servant attitude?

Who would find it easier to serve? Why?

Which person likes to control other people?

Why would A prefer to associate with C, rather than B?

What happens when two A people try to relate to each other?

Two C's?

Which person does not want the responsibility of self-esteem?

Which person uses others for his own convenience?

Which person needs constant reassurance?

Which person feels a need to put others down?

Which person is most likely to make a real commitment to another person?

Who is most apt to want close fellowship with God?

Who is most able to sustain close fellowship with God?

In answers to questions like these lies the pain of relationships. If we cannot relate to ourselves, how can we relate to others? If we are unwilling to be who we are and accept ourselves, warts and all, what are we saying about being made in the image of God, about being human? Our confusion goes back to the Fall, to the self-contradiction of Adam and Eve. We must take seriously both the image of God in us and the profound consequences of the Fall, because both are truth. Life is imperfect, and we are fallen, but we still bear the image of God.

Second only in importance to our view of God is our view of self. In one sense, the two go together. Phillips Brooks wisely said, "The true way to be humble is not to stoop until you are smaller than yourself but to stand at your real height against some higher nature that will show you what the real smallness of your greatness is." If we have a God who is *big enough* (El Shaddai) then we can be who we are, admitting weaknesses and finding solutions in him. All our relationships depend on this.

### Rescued from the Outside

Where do we find self-esteem? In the heart of the God who made us and in relating to the God who loves us. He already knows all about us, so no cover-up job is necessary. He will never discover anything about us that will surprise him. His love is utterly realistic; we cannot disillusion him. He *loves* us.

Why do we need self-esteem? To be able to love God properly in return. Only then will we find that our joy does not hinge upon ourselves but upon God, the source of all good. No more personal towers of Babel, our attempts to make a name for ourselves; God is the only worthy object of our praise.

God's love for us is almost too good to believe. Some choose not to believe it—that is their right as human beings. While some are trying to get rid of the shabbiness that makes them ashamed in God's presence, others are working on an independent super-self; both are mired in self's efforts.

Still God's love persists. He could have simply chosen to write us off, but his love did quite the opposite. He chose instead to restore our relationship to himself. Our dear Welsh friend, Elwyn Davies, put it like this:

We are fallen, but not forsaken;
We are fallible, but not expendable;
We are unworthy, but not worthless.

To restore us to fellowship God had to take care of sin, that raging hostility against his holiness. He cannot deny his own nature as we have done. His justice and his holiness demand that what is wrong be put right. A death sentence hangs over condemned mankind, and a penalty must be paid.

## Operation Rescue

So begins the story of the Great Descent from heaven that we celebrate at Christmas time. The plan of redemption that God announced to Eve (Genesis 3:15) goes into operation. God, in the Person of the Son, comes to earth as a human being, conceived in the virgin Mary and born as a baby in Bethlehem. He is named Jesus "because he will save his people from their sins" (Matthew 1:21). He grows to manhood, understanding and experiencing our world. He demonstrates how to live a perfect life in an imperfect world, and in doing so he exposes our failure. He shows us what God is like. No man can lay a charge against him, yet wicked men crucified him because they loved their own ways more than his. His death was not a mistake on the pages of history; it was no martyrdom. Hanging on the cross in what seemed to be utter ignominy and shame in the eyes of those he created, he was bearing the guilt of the world, dying the death that was our due. God was in the hands of man, but with an eternal purpose, a cosmic significance; his death is not the end of the story, but only the beginning.

Today (oh, how we love telling this story) he draws all men to him, as he said he would. He stretches out his hands in love and says, "Come to me, all you who are weary and burdened, and I will give you rest" (Matthew 11:28). There is rest from the burden of guilt and forgiveness for sins, rest from wandering in the land of Nod, rest from inadequacy and confusion and fear of death. He gives those who come to him eternal life and the security of belonging to him, of having a place already prepared in heaven. He draws those who love him near to his side and gives them the inestimable privilege of knowing him.

What awesome freedom there is *to become* in love like this.

And it isn't just because I am loved; it is because of *who* it is that loves me. He declared my worth when he died for me, and now he wants me to participate more and more in his nature. All self's needs are met in his love. When we know him, we have come home. There is nothing left to prove; we can concentrate now on knowing him and becoming like him. Somehow being loved always gives a person room to grow, in relationship to himself and in relationship to others.

## A Climate of Love

Because God loves, we, too, can love. We have two verbs: like and love, but with incredible carelessness we misuse both and endow them with little meaning. We say we love lemon pie and sports cars, and in the same breath say we love our children and love God.

God is not so fickle. His love is without selfish gain. It is a commitment, not a passing fancy. He wants us to know that kind of love and bathe in its luxury until it overflows to others. C. S. Lewis writes, "Our whole being by its very nature is one vast need; incomplete, preparatory, empty yet cluttered, crying out for Him who can untie things that are now knotted together and tie up things that are dangling loose."[6] The love of God shown in Christ Jesus is the most untangling and uncluttering thing we will ever know.

When God redeems a person, he purposes to do a complete job, aiming to redeem every part of life, not just the soul. (The phrase "soul-winner" does not express the completeness that God is after.) Some people only want Christ as a ticket to heaven; they don't want to be changed, to be made holy, or even to be healed. It is easier to keep the closets shut and the doors to some parts of life barred completely, or so they think. It allows private indulgence and self-pity, and it also encourages fear and the very unreality that Christ came to change. That is not salvation; it is unbelief. It denies both God's grace and his love.

But Christ will have none of that. He is not only Savior; he is Lord. He wants to redeem our self-view, our sexuality, our appetites, our minds, our relationships, so that we begin to think like Christians. He accepts us as we are, forgives our sins, gives us eternal life—and then he begins very practically to process the troubled areas of our lives. He provides a climate of acceptance, so that in working together—you and God—change can take place. It is a divine partnership. It may not be a quick cure, for some of our habits have deep roots, but healing and redemption are assured because of the character of God.

Our private little sins are the ones that nip at our spiritual growth. (Is there such a thing as a *private* or a *little* sin?) Most of these have their roots in the *self* problem we have been talking about, so that we waste our energy defending ourselves, blaming others, and avoiding our relationships. We may or may not be responsible for the past, but we are responsible for the present. Every day we make choices. Will we give up this "private little sin" to God and trust him, working with him for victory, or will we continue to carry our own baggage? It is as simple and as complicated as that; it is as full of agony and joy as that; it is as vulnerable and safe as that, because God is in on it.

### Trust vs. Fear

A tension exists between fear and trust in our lives. It can be diagrammed like this:

Fear ←——————————————→ Trust

Trusting God is what the Christian life is really all about. We vacillate between trust and fear as if we were riding on a teeter-totter. Fear either paralyzes us or causes us to rush in and take matters into our own hands as if we were orphans in the universe, while trust, on the other hand, lets God be in charge, talks things over with the Father, and *rests* with him.

Trust is not a magic talisman that you wear around your neck. It is not superstition or wishful thinking like "I trust it won't rain." Neither is it blind faith, without substance or content. Trust is a certainty because of Who we are trusting, not because we know the end of the matter.

Personal trust in God is like a cord made up of three strands, involving 1) informed thinking, 2) humble thinking, and 3) an obedient will.[7]

*Informed thinking* means we must know who God is, what he is like, and what he has done in human history, which is why the Scriptures are so important. We read the Old Testament and hear Joshua tell the children of Israel that one of them can rout a thousand when God fights for him. We rehearse the marvelous acts of God in history. We read of his holiness, his goodness, his severity, his mercy—all his attributes in perfect harmony. We say with the psalmist, "This God is our God for ever and ever; he will be our guide even to the end" (Psalm 48:14).

*Humble thinking* means not thinking we know more than God. It lets God be God and remembers that he said his ways are higher than our ways and his thoughts higher than our thoughts (Isaiah 55:9). How inappropriate, then, to say, "My idea of God . . ." or "I can't imagine a God who . . ." or worse still, "If I were God . . ." Humble thinking means that we defer to him the details of life we can't understand—the baby born with severe handicaps, the father of five children killed last week, and all our "unanswered prayers." When life doesn't go our way, it is easy to be arrogant and impatient, to think God may need a little help from us, but that is the opposite of humble thinking.

An *obedient will* means that there will be tension, that other options are present that lure us. We must choose, and the choice has moral significance. Life is full of options: green tie, red tie; Burger King or Charley's Pizza Hut; Route 66 or Highway 75. In and of themselves these have no moral significance. The test of an obedient will comes not in a vacuum, but when the pressure is on, when the choices affect our relationship to God and to others. *To lie or not to lie, to cheat or not to cheat, to pilfer company property or not.*

Genuine trust has all three of these strands—informed thinking, humble thinking, and an obedient will. Our personal trust in God must be woven into the fibers of our being so that our whole self is resting solidly on the person of God.

Trust goes beyond feelings, beyond fear, and becomes the means for realizing God's redemption in every part of life. How does it work? Let us take an example that has bearing upon relationships.

God wants to redeem our self-view and free us from self-absorption. He has accepted us and restored us. The implication of this must be worked out in our lives. Suppose Ruth has struggled with a poor self-view. She hasn't been to college, and her associations are now largely with people who are college graduates. They haven't noticed her lack, but she feels it strongly. When discussions with these acquaintances become spirited and interesting, Ruth retreats in fear, even though she has ideas she wants to share. Afterward she feels annoyed with others and with herself because she is sure that she had as much to offer as they did, but she felt inadequate and said nothing. Why? She is intimidated by her fears. They are educated; she is not. What would they have thought of her opinions? She resents others for running all over her with their ideas, but every time she allows fear to silence her.

We suggest that Ruth evaluate her trust in God. Can he give her a sense of propriety about her contributions in conversation, and can he help her verbalize adequately? Ruth has a choice: will she fear or trust? To the extent that she trusts God, she reaches out and becomes a freer person, one who is more sure of her identity. That is the practical stuff out of which identity develops. Ruth has a choice about two ways to act: one is fear, which is self-defeating, the other is trust, which is an affirmation of her relationship with God and thus of herself.

Does it sound too simple? Will we trust or fear? Unless we know God, trust seems a bigger risk than fear. Fear drives us back to seek the safety of some mysterious womb. Change is frightening; return to a safe place. But the womb is an illusion; we can't go back. We can only stay immature and confused if we don't get into the stream of life by trusting. It can be illustrated by the diagram on the following page.

The upward curve represents the maturing life. Above the line are steps of positive growth; below the line are the negatives. Trust moves a person into identity. Fear only intensifies confusion about self and life. Identity moves a person toward intimacy, which is the ability to know and be known by another person. On the underside of the line, confusion leads to isolation and the utter loneliness where fear thrives.[8]

We have a deep longing for intimacy. We are relational beings, propelled by an inner drive toward others. It is possible to seek intimacy without identity, but seeking is not finding. Note that the opposite of identity is confusion. When confused people involve themselves in the lives of others, deep hurts often result.

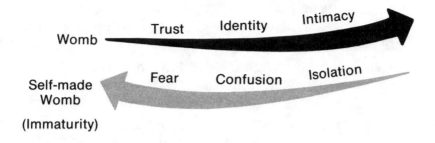

There are no short cuts; all relationships are built on trust. Our relationship with God begins that way, and it flourishes as we persist in trusting. That relationship is rather like what Aslan, the golden-maned lion of Narnia, once said to Lucy in C. S. Lewis's book *Prince Caspian*: "Every year you grow you will find me bigger."

---

[1] Helmut Thielicke, *How the World Began* (Stuttgart, Germany: Muhlenberg Press, 1960), 203. In striking contrast to Abel's blood, the blood of Jesus cries out in grace. Hebrews 12.24: ". . . Jesus the mediator of a new covenant, and to the sprinkled blood that speaks a better word than the blood of Abel."

[2] Derek Kidner, *Genesis, An Introduction and Commentary* (London: Tyndale Press, 1967), 76.

[3] Ibid., 78.

[4] Thielicke, *How the World Began*, 230.

5Stanley Coopersmith, *The Antecedents of Self Esteem* (San Francisco: W. H. Freeman and Company, 1967), 46, 48.

6C. S. Lewis, *The Four Loves* (New York: Harcourt, Brace and Company, 1960), 14.

7Derek Kidner, *Psalms* (London: InterVarsity Press, Tyndale Old Testament Commentary, 1976), 282.

8Material adapted from Erik H. Erikson, *Identity, Youth and Crisis* (New York: W. W. Norton and Co., Inc., 1968), 95.

*chapter* 3

# Who Knows Who You Are?

*Time* magazine did a cover story on the actor Peter Sellers shortly before he died at age fifty-four. *Time* quoted one of his friends as saying, "Peter is the accumulation of all the roles he's played and all the people he's met. He's directing traffic inside all that." When Sellers appeared on *The Muppets*, Kermit the frog told him just to "relax and be yourself," to which Sellers replied, "I could never be myself. You see, there is no me. I do not exist." The *Time* writer concluded, "It reveals his profound fear that the real Peter Sellers is virtually a cipher, that he has no personality and that he will either not be able to find or will at the last minute lose whatever fictive creation he has chosen to wrap around himself."[1]

We didn't know Peter Sellers, but we know people like him who have been playing roles all their lives, who are on stage even when they are alone in a room. That makes it difficult to know who they are! A minister's wife laughingly told us that she walked down a deserted church hallway smiling so brightly that her face hurt. When she realized what she was doing, she stopped and said aloud to no one, "Why am I doing this?" She was playing her role without the benefit of an audience.

Many people aren't the least bit introspective. They use up their days without ever wondering who they are. Others may long to have someone really know and understand them, but hiding behind masks and submerging the real self over the years makes knowing oneself more scary and difficult. Unfortunately the masks we put on to keep us from being found out also keep us from being found. The "hat" I wear can slip over my face and become a mask. Psychologists say this is probably what midlife crisis is all about—the need to know oneself before dying.

God makes each of us a unique human being—not clones. He encourages us to discover who we are, and we cannot truly know ourselves except through the process of disclosing ourselves to others.

## Self-Disclosure

What do we mean by self-disclosure? We do not mean dumping the file drawers of your life on everyone you meet. That is an inappropriate self-disclosure. We are talking about the willingness to be known, the willingness to share feelings, ideas, fears, doubts, past experiences, and future hopes with the confidence that what you are and what you think will benefit the life of someone else. Each person will do this differently because temperament, emotional expressiveness, and verbal skills differ, but the willingness to be known still evidences itself.

Disclosing yourself to another corrects the inaccuracies of introspection. What we mull over privately has a different look when exposed. When we bounce our perceptions off another person, what comes back to us has a correcting, uplifting influence.

And when deep personal contact occurs with another, language and images are suddenly clearer. The climate changes. The talk becomes more spontaneous. We tell stories from our lives and give illustrations with new freedom. We have flashes of insight and moments of transparency. We experience relationship and realize that *this* is what gives life meaning.

That is what we've been discussing in the preceding chapters—discovering who we are so we can be ourselves and experience serenity and joy in knowing God and others. It is as though God were spinning out an overlapping spiral of grace as he shows us *himself* and reveals new truths about our *selves*; all the while we learn from sharing in *another's* life and see more of God and self. Simultaneously, the circle becomes bigger and bigger. It is called *growing*. No matter how mature we become, there are always new truths to learn about ourselves and our relationships. The maturing person is always processing the events of his or her life.

All of us are an impenetrable mystery—even to ourselves. We are always making new discoveries about self. How wrong, then, to act as if we knew all about another person, as if there were nothing new to be learned and no dimension of personhood to explore, as if there were a person on the shelf marked *Known Quantity*. That is foreclosing on a person.[2] This is an affront to the divinely created personality of another, especially when we must admit that we don't completely know our own selves.

We make decisions about people all the time based on prejudice, insecurity, and lack of information. Labels and stereotypes are cruel because people are living, not static; there are many shades and nuances in understanding another person. We believe this is true about ourselves, so why wouldn't it be true about others? No one wants to be summed up by a label.

Author Gore Vidal once commented that when he meets a person at a party who seems dull and uninteresting, he asks himself, "What makes this person so boring?" which gets him so interested in knowing the person that he finds himself fascinated. He says there is no such thing as a boring person—only people who have to be discovered because they don't know how to tell you who they are!

We see around us people who have never let themselves be known, who have never practiced self-disclosure. And it is fair to say that there is a lack of "humanness" about some of them, a brittle quality that cares more about structure, efficiency, and success than about living people. To be human is to be involved with other people, and not just superficially, but in depth. There is both fear and pain in the Simon and Garfunkel song,

> I touch no one and no one touches me,
> I am a rock, I am an island,
> And a rock feels no pain, and an island never cries.

But no man is an island; we do touch, and within us there is a legitimate longing to belong, to know and be known, that is called intimacy. Only fear—the basis of all anxieties—keeps us from experiencing such communion with another.

### Intimacy and Growth

What is intimacy? The word comes from the Latin *intimare*, "to make known" and *intimus*, "innermost." It is a close personal relationship marked by affection and love in which people reveal their inner characters and truest selves. When it is defined, words like *openness, honesty, mutual self-disclosure, caring, warmth, protected, committed, transparency,* and *attachment* are used.

Intimacy may seem to be a feminine prerogative, and many believe that "women are the undisputed intimacy specialists in our society."[3] Little boys train to take roles in which displays of emotions are considered inappropriate, while little girls prepare for roles of mothering and nurturing, and practice being intimate with girl friends as they grow up. Many young women who are prepared for intimacy experience severe disappointment when they meet men who know little about it.

Men have the same need for intimacy as women, even though they often have less experience. Intimacy is a *human* need and is not based on gender. Recent changes in our society have made the need for intimacy more intense for both sexes. Men are beginning to discuss freely the need for close friendships and more intimate relationships. Success in other endeavors has not brought the rewards that satisfy deep inner needs. They want a close relationship with their children, but they don't know how to go about it. This disturbs them about parenting. Men tend to turn to women to meet their intimacy needs and are intimacy-takers rather than intimacy-givers. Intimacy is necessary for human survival; it is also necessary for a full sense of personhood.

Healthy people are both *interdependent* and *independent*. These two traits are important in understanding intimacy. If we overvalue independence, we undervalue relationships. The super-independent person says, "I don't need anyone; I can handle that myself." Independent people often have trouble even accepting love. Yet everyone needs love and needs to love. The person who prides himself on being independent may have trouble with both.

Pity the newly widowed woman who refuses dinner invitations because she doesn't want to be dependent on others. She ends up eating Christmas dinner alone because others grew tired of inviting. What seemed to her a show of strength and independence became instead the cultivation of loneliness. Another man lay on the linoleum floor of his apartment kitchen for two days before anyone heard his feeble call. As a result of his independence hardly anyone knew him well enough to miss him.

We trap people into a wrong kind of independence by the way we treat them. In our enchantment with success and celebrities, we sometimes make a person a *mogul*—a hero whose feet hardly touch the ground—and build a mystique around that person that does not allow for common human feelings and failure. Leo Buscaglia commented in a magazine interview that he feels uneasy whenever someone writes, "I'm a fan of yours." He writes back immediately, "Please don't be a fan. Be a friend." Friends allow you to be who you are; fans have expectations. Their expectations set a person up for unreality and can foster fear of close relationships. On the other hand, we do the same to the ordinary people in our lives when we stereotype them instead of insisting that they grow. We say, "Aunt Sara is so independent," and excuse her from responsibility in relationships. Aunt Sara continues to cultivate loneliness, but whether or not she admits it, she needs us.

Interdependence is a different matter. It is not dependency—one person leaning on another, but rather, it means each needing the other. The image is not two people propping each other up, but two people arm-in-arm accomplishing tasks and living life. We are called not to dependency *on* others, but to responsibility *for* others.

You are independent in that you stand in your own skin, responsible to be who you are and responsible for all your choices. No one can be *you* for you. You are accountable to become the person God made you to be, but no one can know himself in isolation. We cannot begin to experience life or understand who we are without each other. In that sense we are interdependent, having a common vulnerability in life that urges us toward intimacy.

Intimacy is not dependency. Intimacy always means taking the risk to let yourself be known. The more certain you are of your personal identity, the more courage you have to risk being open with others. Intimacy is essential for personal growth—whether it is with God or fellow human beings. When you give someone transparent glimpses into you, you also *see* and better understand yourself. Somehow you free yourself from the prison of fear of what others will think about you. Growth comes from facing reality and seeing what is really there. Only then are people open for love and new healing.

In the parable of the prodigal son (Luke 15:11–32), the younger son appears to scorn intimacy and interdependence with his father and goes to a distant country. The older son appears to value intimacy and remains at home, busy in the father's affairs. Both, in fact, kept control over their own lives, and neither had an open, warm relationship with their father. The test comes for the younger son when physical need drove him to come "to his senses" and admit his need for his father. He repents, confesses, and returns to find the father waiting. He exposes his inner feelings and willingness for a servant relationship only to discover how much his father desired him to be his *son*.

The older brother observes the reunion celebration from afar. His relationship with his father was such that he did not come to him to make inquiry about the merrymaking. He went to a servant instead. His response of anger further shows how far his heart was from his father's and how alone the older brother really was—cut off from both his father and his brother. But, like the father in the story, God allows people today to live within the prison of their own choices and remain independent and unknown.

That is why the tragedies in our lives can help us grow. They have the potential to open us up to new feelings, to think honest thoughts, to share our hurts with others, to be "unclothed" before God. It depends on how we respond. Some people make a second tragedy out of their response. Reuel Howe has commented that every day something happens that either results in the growth of the soul or the diminishing of the soul, and it is our willingness to process what happens that makes the difference. Pain stops us in our tracks and reminds us that we need to interpret what is taking place in our lives.

These same principles apply in relating to God, *the living God*, not some concept or vague principle. When approaching him, some wear the same masks they wear in public or devise new ones that have a holy aura. Do we think we can fool God? We cannot draw near if we won't present our real selves to him. What kind of spiritual buffoonery that is! We can only know God intimately by being radically open with him. Remember, he will never discover anything about us that will surprise him. No heart-warming music, religious programming, or sentiment can give us the kind of intimacy that will assure us that we are fully known and loved. Only the courage to lay all that we are out before him can do that. Religious life that lacks intimacy with God is hollow ritual. God has taken the initiative in self-disclosure, and we need to listen to him as well as talk with him. Intimacy is not a monologue.

## Equipped to Communicate

God has equipped us for relationships. We are naturally gifted. We can use language, for example. We mentioned being word-partners with God earlier. We take the symbols known as words and use them to share a variety of experiences, to describe places to people who have not been there, or friends they have not met. We express not merely facts, but emotions and ideas. We create a world for someone else to live in with speech as surely as God spoke and created the world in the beginning. We make home either a haven or a misery by the way we talk to each other. People are built up or destroyed by words. This should give us a bit of awe about language.

Language and thought are integrated; each shapes the other. Our word choices mold our outlook on life. Speech is important. On the other hand, our life-view can determine our choice of words. Language denotes a certain carefulness about life and the people in it. We are stewards of words. That is why the Bible makes such a point about speech— that it be honest, that it edify, that it be gracious, but not insipid. It is to be seasoned with salt.

Just because we can talk doesn't mean we know how to communicate. Communication involves being significantly in touch with another person. When two people really *meet*, it is because they each transcend themselves. A person reaches outside of himself to experience more than he is.

Communication is a matter of life or death to people either outwardly or inwardly. The teenager who grunts minimal answers to his parents is more than disrespectful; he is destructive. Someone has reached out to him as a person, but he has not responded as a person. The silent father who never shares ideas or who does not instruct or affirm his family with his speech does not get out of his responsibility by defining himself as a "quiet person." He may just be lazy. We have the gift of speech; it is a responsibility to use this gift and use it wisely.

Language overkill is a problem of another kind. Some people think everything has to always be said all the time. Such loquaciousness stems from the same fear that keeps another person silent, and it does not qualify as communication. Communication is more than talking; it is being heard and understood. It must be mutual; it must proceed from both sides with persistence borne out of a desire to be understood. Otherwise it is a monologue, not a dialogue.

In her book *Peoplemaking*, Virginia Satir makes this bold claim for communication: "I see communication as a huge umbrella that covers and affects all that goes on between human beings. Once a human being has arrived on this earth, communication is the largest single factor determining what kinds of relationships he makes with others and what happens to him in the world about him."[4]

Speech is only one part of communication. Body language also communicates. The meaning is clearest when the mouth and the body are saying the same thing. Mixed messages get inaccurate readings. A look, an expression, a posture, a movement of the hands, a tone of voice—we say so much with our whole person. Communication involves the total person.

We are gifted to communicate, and we are responsible to communicate. We must believe this is essential to our humanity and then get on with the responsibility of properly using the gift. "Communication is really the attempt on the part of two selves to find and to call each other out of the loneliness of independent selfhood into a relationship of mutual interest and purpose. The establishment of a relationship is not easy. Two individuals are like two impregnable fortresses. They cannot be taken by assault."[5] There is an advance and withdrawal rhythm in our relationships. We reach out, we retreat. Each must build a bridge to the other, and that bridge is communication and can be defined as the real person inside one individual getting in touch with the real person inside another individual.

Picture two people—Joe and Pete. Each is a solitary being, but each is made for relationship. What must happen for this relationship to take place? One must speak; the other must listen.

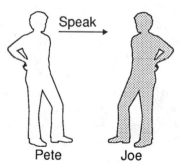

Speak →

Pete          Joe

Figure 3.1

Pete initiates; he must speak meaningfully and responsibly. Joe listens. Listening is the most important aspect of relationship. Thoreau once said, "It takes two to speak a truth; the one to speak, the other to listen." And the burden for understanding is on the listener.

How does Joe listen? Does he listen with prejudice? ("I cannot hear you because of what I expect you to say.") Does he listen with anger or with fear? With insecurity? Our attitude can keep us from hearing. If Joe listens with compassion and understanding, Pete will feel he is heard, and then genuine communication begins to form the bridge between them. No matter how the relationship turns out, no one can be a loser when this affirming activity takes place. This kind of listening is a gift we give one another; it is a form of love.

## No Relationship Without Communication

Communicating is not an easy task, even though it is a human function. Barriers exist because we are fallen people. Overcoming these barriers makes communication an adventure that builds patience, stamina, and persistence—and strengthens all the muscles of the personality. It is not simply the sending and receiving of the content of messages. If it were, someone would have mastered and formalized the process years ago. Communication involves relationships between human beings, and sometimes it seems that we understand very little of what it means to be human. We can begin to understand by focusing on three aspects of communication: the inexactness of language, how anxiety can spoil communication, and how the past and present affect communication.

### Language is not always exact

Words or phrases have been given different meanings in different families or in other associations. Behind the words exists a whole life of relationships out of which meanings come. The use of the word *father*, for example, brings a special image and emotional feeling to each person. One person may have a warm, safe feeling while another hears the word with a nervous, negative feeling in the pit of the stomach. Words conjure up images. We have to check to see if our meanings match. The communicator does have the burden to make his meanings as clear as possible so the listener can process them. Yet both speaker and listener must be open to each other's meanings and inquire about what is unclear. In that sense we need to police our communications.

People can talk together for some time before realizing they aren't discussing what they thought they were. One man thought they were going to "raise" a wall while the other thought they were going to "raze" the wall. We need to police our communications by asking, "This is what I heard; is that what you meant?" As C. S. Lewis once said, "We had better not follow Humpty Dumpty in making words mean whatever we please."

The light dawned on a couple in a one-day marriage enrichment seminar when they made a surprising discovery about their communication patterns. She grew up in a family that gave second-level messages or messages with implied meanings. The mother would say, "The garbage needs to be taken out," and someone knew they were being asked to take out the garbage. He grew up in a family in which the members said what they meant with no hidden messages or agendas. The young wife followed her mother's pattern by dropping hints. The husband thought she was giving interesting information and not making a request—even though he might have been able to guess why she pouted so much. She pouted because she thought he didn't love her enough to do what she asked; she never realized that she hadn't really asked him to do anything.

*Communication can also be spoiled by anxiety*

One person has "agenda anxiety" and pours out his message without checking to see if he is understood. In turn the listener may not really listen. Perhaps the listener has his own agenda and is waiting for his turn to speak. Other anxieties keep people from hearing or communicating accurately—personal problems, time pressures, illness or other discomforts, or uneasy feelings about the subject matter of the conversation.

Threatened people can hear the strangest messages out of fear or a sense of inadequacy. It is the old game of "You said . . ." with the listener thinking "I never made a statement like that in all my life!"

If we listen or speak defensively or with prejudice, we spoil communication before it even begins. An affirming listener answers ideas with ideas and feelings with feelings. The defensive listener confronts a feeling with an idea or an idea with a feeling. Think about how that frustrates genuine communication. You feel deeply about something that has happened and want to discuss the feeling, but the other person shifts the conversation to cold facts, leaving you feeling very misunderstood and lonely. Or the opposite occurs: You want to discuss the facts and the other person keeps throwing in feelings; this clouds the issue and leaves you feeling misunderstood and confused. Or one person discusses *what* is right, and the other discusses *who* is right, and both think they are talking about the same subject!

Listening means focusing on the one who is speaking and hearing the meaning behind what is being said. A certain kind of listening reaches into the other person's heart and affirms that person. It is a selfless function to listen.

*Communicating from the past and the present*

When Pete speaks, he communicates from two aspects of his life: his past history and his present life. Both of these give the meaning to his words and the ideas he expresses. His past history includes his family background, the traditions and beliefs that have influenced him—the sum total of his experiences, and his vocabulary reflects his past. His contemporary life involves what he does, what he reads, who he meets, his associations—all that makes up the values of his contemporary life.

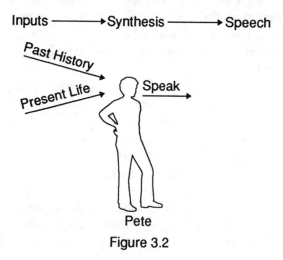

Pete

Figure 3.2

Pete must correlate his past and his present life if he wants his communication to be clear. Otherwise he sends out a mixed message, and he listens with unresolved vibrations from his already spoken words that blur what he hears. The message and the listening represent what is happening to him on the inside.

Let us imagine Pete has an inner storehouse full of anger from accumulated injustices and misunderstandings from his relationship with his father. He's kept the door closed on his feelings and scarcely admits their presence because "you aren't supposed to feel that way about your father." His anger remains with him; he never dealt with it. In his contemporary life he relates poorly to all authority figures. His anger leaks out around the edges. He is a perfectionist in his work to "show him," but he gets little joy from his performance and may quit his job on what seems like a whim. He does not hear what others say. His communication is marked with hostility that bears no relationship to the present situation. Pete is bent all out of shape. He needs to integrate his past and present because he can neither listen nor communicate in his personal relationships the way things stand.

Traditions and beliefs that have been deeply ingrained in our thinking cannot be ignored, either. The past needs to be integrated or processed into one's current lifestyle. Suppose you grew up in a family where almost all purchases were paid for in cash and saving was important—"Laying something aside for a rainy day!" was a maxim you wanted to live by. Then you marry someone who handles money differently, who uses credit generously, and who is not concerned about saving—"Enjoy it now; pay for it later" is his motto.

You have conflicting strains in your life that need integrating. Otherwise you will vacillate between one idea and the other, and your communication within marriage will reflect this inner confusion. Your spouse will have difficulty understanding your guilt feelings and your lack of joy over generosity. Words like "spendthrift" or "penny-pincher" will be thrown around without adequate definition and will be used as accusations, not well-intended descriptions. Often the issues are far more complicated than this and involve resentments, deep hurts, misunderstandings, and lack of forgiveness—all of which are harder to work through.

How does a person begin to integrate his past and his present? Essentially a person asks, "Why do I think and act the way I do?" Counselors help people answer that question on a professional basis. You may find the help you need by working through the following evaluations.

1. *Think through the values given you.*
   Where did these come from?
   Which values are valid today?
   What is appropriate expression of these values?
   How do these shape your future?

2. *Evaluate your past relationships.*
   Which have given you a sense of affirmation?
   Which have hurt you?
   How are these either aiding or crippling your present life?

3. *Look at your fears.*
   Where did these come from?
   How are you expressing them?
   Which are legitimate and which are excess baggage you need to dispose of?
   How will you dispose of unwanted fears?

4. *What are your dreams and hopes?*
   Which are desirable?
   Which are realistic in light of your present situation? Your potential situation?
   How do these relate to your present contentment?

We need to dialogue within ourselves to straighten out what we really think and what our values really are, and that takes courage. But we can also be correlating as we communicate. Another person can help us make sense out of what is happening inside. A person who is integrating his life is fun to dialogue with because something is happening in his life that stimulates something in ours.

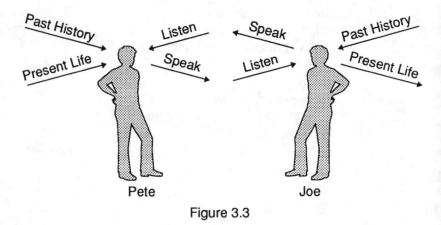

Figure 3.3

Joe, on the other end of the relationship, listens from the vantage point of his past history and his contemporary life. What he hears Pete say is conditioned by these two factors. When he speaks, his meanings will reflect how well he has correlated his past and his present life. Somehow both Pete and Joe must make their meanings meet if real communication is to take place. Each will speak; each will listen. It can be illustrated in the following way.

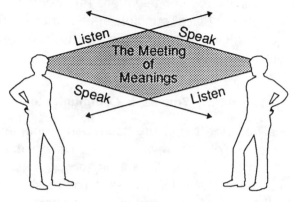

**Figure 3.4**

Where their lines cross—in that small diamond-shaped segment in the center—is the point at which they have understood each other. Both may have said more than was really heard or heard more than was really said, but where their meanings connected, the real person of one met the real person of the other, and genuine dialogue or communication took place. The "meeting of meanings" is what communication is all about.[6]

Dialogue does not always mean agreement or even a sharing of the same goals. Polarity can be a resource that enriches both lives, like iron sharpening iron. But our meeting of meanings shrinks to the degree that fear, anger, prejudice, pride, and language block our communication. That we can relate to each other in this fallen world and have our real persons *meet* is a miracle. We wonder that it ever happens at all. When it does, it is always accompanied by a special touch of the grace of God.

All communication is a team effort. This is true in all

human relationships: parents and children; teachers and students; minister and congregation. The method may be a lecture, but the dialogical principle applies if any meaning is communicated. It takes two to speak a truth: one to speak and the other to listen.

## Where Are You as a Communicator?

Your initial reaction to all this talk about communications and the "meeting of meanings" may be to groan and say that it sounds too hard or that it is a bit too egg-headish. Who wants to analyze everything you say? You've lived this long without falling apart because of poor communication, so why bother now?

Our goal in sharing these ideas is not to burden or stress you but to encourage your own understanding of who you are and how you communicate yourself. Most problems in human relationships relate to self-view and communication skills, and how you handle these ideas depends on how much you value relationships.

Everyone needs to be known. The safe warmth of being accepted and understood by someone meets a genuine human need. Some people tell their dog more about themselves than they tell another person, which may offer its own comfort, but it lacks human responsibility and the risk of relationships. It lacks that for which we were made!

And we have more to communicate than simply ourselves. A whole world of ideas and thoughts—enough to delight and stimulate into eternity—is waiting to be talked about and shared. Ideas about truth, the meaning of life, knowing God, good and evil, joy and sorrow, and the Good News. Don't you want to share some of these with someone?

[1] Richard Schickel, "Peter Sellers," *Time*, (3 March 1980), 64.

[2] From a seminar by Reuel Howe on *Creative Aging* given in Ann Arbor, Michigan, in 1982. Reuel Howe has written *Man's Need and God's Action*, *The Creative Years*, and *The Miracle of Dialogue* (Seabury Press). He is part director of the Institute of Advanced Pastoral Studies in Birmingham, Michigan. Now retired, he is a lecturer and seminar leader on topics related to material in his books.

[3] Rubenstein and Shaver, *In Search of Intimacy* (New York: Delecorte Press, 1982), 24.

[4] Virginia Satir, *Peoplemaking* (Palo Alto, Calif.: Science and Behavior Books, Inc., 1972), 30.

[5] Reuel Howe, *The Creative Years* (Greenwich, Conn.: Seabury Press, 1959), 69.

[6] Adapted from Reuel Howe, *The Miracle of Dialogue* (Greenwich, Conn.: Seabury Press, 1963), 46.

*chapter* 4

# Sexuality and Relationships

The God-created goodness of sexuality and its mystery ought to be a source of gladness and well-being for us. Instead, it often poses an enormous threat to our personhood. We are not sure how we feel about our restless urges, these irrational upheavals within us. We can't imagine that God in his holiness even knows about sex, that sexuality could be his idea, and that he thinks sexuality is good.

As a result, the sexual side of our nature is kept in the dark like a favorite hidden toy. It is something God tolerates but surely does not want to discuss with us. Or does he? We aren't certain. We seem to have competing currents flowing through our lives—one so explosive and impulsive that it frightens us, and the other a rational and spiritual "reaching out" for the God who made us. Does all this come from the same spring within us?

## What Is Sexuality?

Our sexuality is intricately woven into the whole of our person. Being a woman is a way for a person to be; being a man is another way for a person to be. Human beings are created in this dual modality, differing from each other and enriching each other by their differences. Sexuality refers to what we are, not only what we do or feel.

Sexuality is physical; it is a matter of hormones and neurology; it is body-life, shape, and form; it is a tension within us; it is male and female. But sexuality is far more than that. It is a drive toward intimacy with another person. We want to share our very self with another, to trust and be trusted, to investigate the mystery of another person and thus the mystery of our own person. Sexuality is an avenue of personal expression, an important way of telling people who we are and what we think and feel. It is the dynamic of our being. It is one of the relationships for which we were made.

Sexuality comes from the mind of the Godhead. Male and female are in his image and meant to experience and reflect something of the union that exists within the Godhead. It is the epitome of communion, and communion is what the image of God is about.[1] Yet quite apart from marriage, we see people blossoming with sexuality, full of the joy and riches of their own perceptions of life. These single people touch other's lives without ever touching their skins, sharing themselves in ways that reflect the image of God.

Sexuality is a powerful entity permeating the way we think, act, walk, talk, and respond. Sex is a function of a person's total self and not just his or her sexual organs. It is hard to define because it spills over into every aspect of our lives. If we would understand ourselves, we must understand how we feel about being sexual, how we value this gift, and how we love and serve God and others as sexual beings.

Some people talk about sexuality as though God manufactured human beings on an assembly line and added the genitals as the last touch before completion, like an ornament on the hood of an automobile: "Let's make this one a man. . . ." That idea makes genitals the only difference between men and women, and it leads to a shabby use of persons. Sex equals genitals; it becomes an act rather than the mystery of knowing another person marvelously different, yet wonderfully similar. To think of male-female relationships only in terms of sex is an insult to our humanity. To view a person as a function, rather than a whole being, is an affront to the God who made us.

Sin disorients and bends sexuality out of shape. Its very dynamic makes sexuality subject to the greatest distortion. Satan has taken the pleasure of the biological dimension of sex and blown it all out of proportion so that intimacy and personhood are all but forgotten. The sex act becomes the pearl of great price. Sexual intercourse, which was meant to express the mysterious union of total person with total person, becomes an extraneous act, the value of which lies in the rapture of the moment. Satan has done a masterful job at confusing people about the meaning of sex, and in doing so he has confused them about their own meaning.

### Redeemed Sexuality

But sexuality—and sexual intercourse—are God's idea, not Satan's. Satan specializes in twisting good things. Whatever is valuable lends itself to counterfeits. *God wants to redeem our sexuality,* our expressions of self, and the games we play with our sexuality along with our feelings about it. He wants to talk over and refine this area of our lives that badly needs His control for maximum expression. He wants to help us handle our passions as those who are made in the image of God for relationships. To be straightforward with God about this is "neither an easy nor a common grace."

God wants a redeemed people to know something of the delight of being sexual persons, of expressing our unique personhood in the world, and of entering into the lives of others with a kind of holy sexual wholeness. He wants a sensuous people ("those readily affected through the senses")—who enjoy the differences in the world—to feel, to think, and to share, instead of being caged by the fear of unchosen urges. His Spirit offers self-control in the areas of passion and desire; he gives a higher calling, a larger view of life. God's love unites a man and a woman in the sacred covenant of marriage to enjoy each other—body, soul, and spirit—and out of that rich love beget children who will know and love God. How fearfully and wonderfully God has made us.

Look at the diagrams on the following page. When we let Christ redeem all parts of our being, we put him in the center where he touches every segment of our lives (diagram A). To have Christ *out of center* is to be eccentric (diagram B).

When Christ is in the center (centric living), the wheel rolls with proper balance, but when he is not in the center (eccentric living), then life bumps along imbalanced. Eccentric living gives way to all sorts of excesses and is essentially non-Christian. Its largest fault is that Christ is not the center but only a segment of life, if he is there at all. If we are made in his image for relationship with him and if he is central, then he must have something to say about every part of life—including the very intimate part, sex.

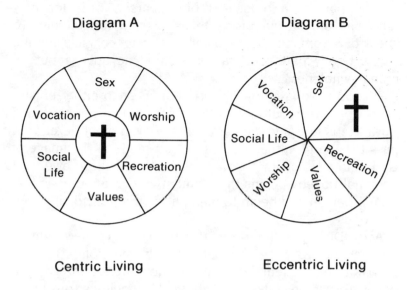

Diagram A — Centric Living

Diagram B — Eccentric Living

How will God redeem our view of sex? He will surely change: 1) the way we view the other person, 2) the way we view our own body, and 3) our understanding of our own sexual urges.

A *redeemed view of others means* we see people as God sees them—made in his image. How do you treat someone made in the image of God? For example, what about that attractive brunette who has the right dimensions in the right places? She is not just a body, nor just a pretty face. Whether *she* knows it or not, *you* know she has been made in God's image with an eternal soul. She is not something to be used either to satisfy ego needs or sexual urges. Potentially she is a sanctuary where God would live through his Holy Spirit.

Our culture is seared by the fires of illicit sexual pleasure and sexual innuendos. Clever suggestive remarks, vulgar language, sexual harassment, naughty little jokes—none of this is part of a redeemed life. Coarse words for holy functions are as inappropriate as pigs in the temple. To speak of a woman as a "good lay" or to refer coarsely about a single bodily part is to say something negative about all human wholeness.

A good-looking fellow is not a conquest to either bolster up a woman's reputation or to assure her of her charming ways. He is not any one part of his body, a meal-ticket, or a pass to a party; rather, he is a person made in the image of God, and that ought to cause more than a little awe. Our personal tragedy begins the moment we see another as less than a person and begin to manipulate the individual to our own ends.

Actor Dustin Hoffman saw this problem in a new light as he practiced playing the part of a woman off screen in preparation for a female role in the movie *Tootsie*. Interviewed on a television talk-show about his feelings on being "feminine," Hoffman said that his most difficult experience was being treated as a nonperson because he was simply a middle-age, very ordinary woman. People chose not to notice him at counters in stores, not to talk to him at social gatherings, and not to offer him courtesies, all of which gave him a new sensitivity to the way people are treated as sexual beings. He found in particular that women are rated by their appearance rather than their person.

A *redeemed view of our own bodies* insures that we will treat them with the respect given to something that belongs to God. The body is not a power tool we use to impress anyone or to get what we want. We need, for example, to ask questions about appropriate modesty regardless of the fashion. In today's society there is no need to wear a bathing suit that covers the knees, but neither must we advertise our flesh with a too-brief bikini. We must ask, "Why do I want to wear this? Who am I pleasing?" That advertising pitch about sex appeal—what is its real message, and what does sex appeal mean? It ought not be a game to arouse someone sexually when such arousal is out of the context of a legitimate relationship. "Sex appeal" may feed ego needs, but it actually reveals more about shallow values and poor self-esteem.

People who respect their bodies do not lend them out for poor use—whether it be drug usage or petting in the back seat of a car or any other kind of experimentation that promises "kicks" in return. People delude themselves about honest behavior in a thousand ways. While some men go from woman to woman, leaving behind professed loves like a basket of bruised fruit, some women clutter their lives with the disrespect of many lovers. Neither of these realize what they are saying about the value of their own persons, that what they call "freedom" is simply license to self-destruction.

*Understanding our sexual urges* necessitates taking our whole person seriously. Our sexual feelings must be integrated with the rest of our life and not be in tandem to it. We are all persons with bodies who need the restraint of our intellect and our spiritual resolve. We do not fence in sexuality to release its hold on our persons; we fence it in because it is part of the scenario of our personal lives.[2]

Sometimes a sexual urge is evidence of insecurity. The man who declares he has a strong sex-drive for which he is not responsible may only be saying that he doesn't know who he is and is desperately trying to find himself. For him sex is exploitation; it is without relationship and thus subject to increasing excesses. He may boast to his peers about his conquests and assume a *macho* role to prove he is someone in his own eyes, but all he has proven is his lack of understanding about what it means to be human.

If a young man feels incompetent in areas of life that test him daily, sexual involvement with a girl may give him control of both a person and a situation. He feels a sense of power found nowhere else in his life. Or often a young woman who longs to be popular gets her sense of worth by attracting men. It is likely that the rise of sexual promiscuity among young people comes from increasing feelings of insecurity and loneliness in our impersonalized, technological society. Suburban and city life offer very little opportunity for the young to prove any capabilities. Carrying out the trash does little for a sense of competence.

Loneliness has been blamed for all kinds of sexual indiscretions. The sex act can create an illusion of closeness and communion, but it cannot take the loneliness out of the person, and in the end, bitterness only drives a person deeper into aloneness. Sexual intercourse is designed to express a oneness that already exists; it cannot create togetherness. Promiscuous people are usually only acting out their personal despair about themselves no matter how liberated they claim to be.

Since God made us sexual beings, we need to understand that our sexual feelings are not wrong in themselves—*it is behavior that matters*. No other area in our lives is so open to exploitation because sexual feelings are not only strong, they are pleasurable. But the sex drive is a cruel tyrant when it is out of control.

Sexual acts involve the whole person no matter how brief the encounter. There is no such thing as casual sex. Paul warns against such sinning against our bodies: "Flee from sexual immorality. All other sins a man commits are outside his body, but he who sins sexually sins against his own body" (1 Corinthians 6:18). The power of sexual feelings leaves us wide open for temptation, but temptation usually comes in through a door left deliberately ajar.

A young woman who came to us for counsel over the years seemed particularly susceptible to sexual sin. She professed to be a Christian, but her sense of personal worth was low. She was subject to depression, had a low view of her body, and lacked discipline in almost every area. She never really seemed to put her faith to work in her life, and in fact, we suspected that she deliberately put herself in compromising situations. She came in tears and repentance one day to tell a very sad story, saying, "I never meant for this to happen." Our question to her was, "Did you intend for it *not* to happen?" That kind of honesty is essential if we are to live out the God-given purpose for our sexuality.

## No Right to Happiness

We actually believe the lies we tell ourselves about our sexual feelings and behavior! We take in the propaganda of the secularists that labels traditional Christian standards "puritanical." (In *The Screwtape Letters*, C. S. Lewis says that the word "Puritan" is certainly one of Satan's "really solid triumphs.") The media says that sex equals happiness, and this idea slowly creeps into our minds. If it were true, then prostitutes would be the happiest and most enviable people in the world. But we don't want to look at sex *that* crassly. Instead, we hear that "the pursuit of happiness" is a basic human right. Yet those who propound the theory seldom talk about the human rights of those abused by others in their pursuit, nor do they recommend that we look at their own lives as a model for the fruit of this pursuit.

Shortly before his death in 1963, C. S. Lewis wrote a disarming essay for *The Saturday Evening Post*, entitled, "We Have No Right to Happiness,"[3] in which he discussed a neighborhood happening. Mr. A deserted Mrs. A and got his divorce to marry Mrs. B, who had likewise deserted Mr. B and got her divorce to marry Mr. A. It was a terrible jumble of hurts and injustice, but Mr. A said, "What could I do? A man has a right to happiness. . . ." The neighbors who observed the depth of their passion for each other could only agree, and not wanting to be judgmental, they said, "They have a right to happiness." "Happiness" here meant simply and solely *sexual happiness*.

People don't talk about that kind of right to happiness in other moral areas. If money makes a robber happy, does that give him the right to rob a bank, and will the depositors say, "Ah, well, he has a right to happiness"? How happy does a drunk driver feel? Certainly the purveyors of the declaration of a fundamental right to happiness did not intend *by any means* to include murder, rape, robbery, treason, or fraud. No society could be built on that basis. Lewis concludes that any "right to happiness" that ignores moral laws must sooner or later destroy us. He says that we have no right to happiness in that sense, but only the right to be happy doing what is right.

That makes clear thinking and personal commitment a critical part of all our relationships. We are not just a large, thumping heart that is caught in the emotional eddy of sexual desire; we are also intellect and will. The whole person needs to act as a whole person—emotion, will, and intellect. It is a lie to say, "This is bigger than both of us," because that is an abdication of what it means to be human. Humans do not copulate by instinct like animals, but rather, they choose their actions.

If someone says, "There's a fire in the house!" what will you do? Your response depends on where the fire is. If it is in the walls, you get out! If the fire is in the furnace, you warm yourself in its comfort. Lust, any inappropriate sexual desire, is a fire in the walls. It is destructive because it seeks only the experience and not the expression of relationship or commitment. Lust wants what it wants *now*; unlike love, it is impatient and selfish and does not seek the highest good of the other. (It is a lie to act as though what *you* want is automatically the other's highest good.) In contrast, love is always concerned with the highest good of the other. Within the framework of love and commitment in marriage, sexual desire is like a fire in the furnace. It is appropriate, full of meaning, and enhances the marriage relationship.

Our culture declares traditional morality obsolete. Television, movies, advertising, books—all are powerful voices telling us that sex is happiness. When people get their moral standards from the media, they are set adrift in a sea of confusion. Self-expression is in; rules are out. "How could anyone possibly know what life is apart from sex?" the culture asks. It is a clever message, because sex has become big business, and propagating the idea that man is made for sex reaps enormous profits for its merchandisers.

When sex is flaunted as recreation, an undisciplined person can easily be trapped, and pornography is part of the trap. None of the men who buy girlie magazines at airport newsstands read them for their intellectual growth, for sexually enticing pictures do not lead to either personal refinement or genuine relationships; they only exploit the person looking at them. And they make the purveyors rich. Pictures, peep shows, stripteases—whatever the allurement—do not satisfy, but only create a thirst for more unreality. Far from being harmless, these pastimes lead a person not only into a kind of bondage, but into self-doubt. Why self-doubt? Because the wrong expression of our sexual urges says so much about the incomplete understanding of our total person.

Jesus was not being a conservative celibate when he warned about the importance of our thought life. (After all, he is the One who created us and knows how we are made!) Outward behavior is not enough. He said, "I tell you that anyone who looks at a woman lustfully has already committed adultery with her in his heart" (Matthew 5:28). "I made a covenant with my eyes," said Job (Job 31:1). It kept him from looking at the wrong things.

Secularists have no concept of a higher being to whom we relate. Since they do not believe that man is made in the image of God, it should not surprise us when they seek alternatives for sexual expression other than biblical ones. One could wish they would be as open in declaring their new ideas bankrupt as they were in espousing them in the first place. George and Nena O'Neill, for example, were interviewed on dozens of talk shows on both radio and television and reviewed in numerous newspapers and magazines when they wrote their book *Open Marriage* in the seventies. Like many similar books, this one caused quite a stir by proposing and elaborating on new sexual freedoms within marriage. However, no publicity accompanied the news that they eventually threw out their own experiment because it turned into bondage and threatened what was really valuable to both of them. Sensible people could see the flaws in their original idea, but the media strains at a gnat and swallows a camel. Even if an idea is ridiculous, the very fact of its elaboration liberalizes the way people think, whether they know it or not.

### Maturing Sexuality

In the process of maturing, boys and girls progress through stages of sexual awareness and relational development. We term these stages:

egocentric— aware of self; seen in young children who are absorbed with their own wants and needs, think the world centers around them, care little about the sex of other children.

homocentric— aware and enjoying relationships with members of their own sex; seen in children through the fourth grade where boys only like boys and girls form special little cliques.

heterocentric— aware of members of the opposite sex, develop friendships and the ability to feel at ease with these friends; usually begins in early years of puberty.

Generally, the age approximations suggested above demonstrate the healthy progression of early development, but years do not automatically cause a person to grow to maturity. Maturity is an upward spiral to new levels of understanding and application. For example, a person is supposed to leave *egocentricity* when he finds out the world is bigger than he is, but some adults have not progressed beyond this stage sufficiently to relate well to either men or women. All fallen human beings fight the tendency to be self-centered, but the emotionally troubled person is absorbed with self's needs and thus is immature.

The homocentric stage has implications that go well beyond early development. Relating to others of your own sex is far more important than most people realize. Because of personal insecurity, this stage is often skipped over completely in the maturing of the late teens and early twenties. A young man, for example, who lacks a sense of his maleness may feel threatened by his male peers because of their challenges, avoid male companionships, and jump prematurely into a comforting friendship with a woman who doesn't threaten his maleness. The same is true for a woman who clings to one man after another without ever having come to terms with others of her own sex. Women threaten her in a way that men do not.

When we skip friendship with others of the same sex, we must then make same-sex friends later if a we are to have a healthy view of ourselves. This is part of the mystery of our sexuality; we understand ourselves as we learn to relate to those who are like us as well as to the opposite sex. We feel this is so important that we warn women about marrying a man who has no male friends. Likewise we tell men to be wary of a woman who has no female friends. It is not an irremediable situation but one that requires great maturity in dealing with the potential problems.

The third stage is heterocentric awareness. We understand this best because we see it all around us—men and women with good relationships and budding relationships in late adolescence. We forget too quickly the pain of learning to be at ease with each other, and we need to be sensitive to those who struggle for years to overcome the fear of heterosexual friendships. It hurts the person who retreats from this stage of growth; it is like missing part of life. Men and women need the rich dimension each brings to a friendship.

### Twisted Sexuality

Coming to terms with sexuality has pitfalls along the way, particularly as a person approaches puberty. As we feel urges we never felt before and as our bodies change, it is possible to get hung up and not mature emotionally through the stages we have just discussed.

One can remain egocentric, absorbed with self. It is hard to invest interest in others when you don't know for sure who you are yourself. Absorption with self can lead to absorption with stimulating oneself sexually. The self-discovery of a child or even an adolescent is different from masturbation as a maturing practice.

Masturbation is widely practiced because it *is* sexually stimulating and can be done in private. That it doesn't involve anyone else is its major problem; it causes a person to withdraw rather than relate. It is a misuse of the gift of sex. Sexuality underscores the importance of relationships; it means reaching out and giving yourself to another. The person who masturbates turns inward and focuses on self.

The second problem with masturbation is that it quickly becomes the master of the one who practices it. Sex is a good servant but a poor master. Sexual feelings are pleasant, and the person soon finds being alone better than being with others. Sexual fantasies involving other people become part of the act. People who are trapped by masturbation usually don't feel good about it.

Thundering judgments about masturbation seem to be a thing of the past. In fact, the practice has been even encouraged by today's liberal sexual mores. Absurd statements are made about feeling at home in your own body and how masturbation is a way to do that, while others say it is a gift of God to encourage continence.

We don't want to be identified with the old wives' tales and the guilt-producing taboos of the past, but we do want to be honest about how we perceive the habit of masturbation. The urgent desire to masturbate gives evidence of an uneasy feeling about oneself; it is tied to self-view. We are so mysteriously interwoven that we cannot separate our sexuality from our total self. Healthy people need to grow in relationships with others rather than hide and comfort their insecurities in the bedroom. When sexual stimulus lacks an interpersonal relationship and commitment to another person, it fosters the very thing it was designed to cure—loneliness.

You are not a sexual time bomb about to explode if there is no sexual release—that is the propaganda of exploiters. No one *has* to masturbate. God did not make your body that way. God created sex for a distinct purpose; it is not a private affair. We instinctively know that the practice is infantile, and we believe that is why there is so much guilt about it. It misses the mark. We need to understand the role of sex in our total picture of life and make decisions accordingly.

Our counseling on this subject had at one time been primarily to male students, but more recently, women students have come to us who were sold the sophisticated idea by another classmate that they should be more familiar with their own bodies, that their bodies were meant to be enjoyed. These women began practicing masturbation and became deeply troubled not only by guilt but by confusion. Each of them discovered that masturbation is a dead-end street leading nowhere and that the practice is counterproductive. Masturbation does not lead to genuine satisfaction, but to withdrawal from others. Interestingly, they felt it did not lead to holiness either. The practice awakens sexual desire, and the repeated refrain in the Song of Songs "Do not arouse or awaken love until it so desires" is profoundly wise.

Bad habits are better not begun. Still, God is in the habit-breaking business. Spend more time with him regularly and less time hating yourself. Sexual feelings aren't wrong; it is what we do with them that matters.

*Homosexuality*

Some people get stuck in the stage of homocentric maturing. They feel ill at ease with the opposite sex, and as a result they are more attracted to members of their own sex. Many of these may be pseudohomosexuals (people who fear they are homosexuals but aren't). But others have a very strong erotic attraction to their own sex, with all the accompanying feelings, that is painful to live with. Yet many never act on those feelings. Instead they make a commitment to chastity. They may never marry, but they live fulfilled, useful, satisfied lives. They may well "renounce marriage because of the kingdom of heaven."

We have trouble calling that kind of person a homosexual, even though the word is widely used to include them. In our definition, a homosexual is one who engages in homosexual acts, acts that result in orgasm between members of the same sex—whether male or female.

The contemporary encouragement of homosexuals to declare they are "gay" has been an attempt to take away any stigma attached to their sexual preference. They define themselves by sexual preference as if that were a total statement of self. A young man went to his priest and told him that he was "gay" and went into great detail to elaborate his feelings about his sexuality. At length the priest said, "Now tell me about yourself. Who are you?" That is the basic question. There are many reasons why this labeling takes place, but you rarely hear anyone define himself by saying, "I am heterosexual."

The problem with a person defining himself or herself as a homosexual is that it tends to take away personal responsibility for one's actions. "That's the way I am; I can't help myself. My nature made me do it. I'm a homosexual." That is not how the Bible refers to our sexuality. It is a gift for which we are responsible. It would be truer to say I am a person with homosexual feelings or whatever. You are not your feelings.

We do not understand why some people have erotic feelings for their own sex, as if they got stuck in the maturing process. In his book *Eros Defiled*, psychiatrist John White writes, "Science has searched in vain to find a physical basis for homosexuality. The testes of male homosexuals produce the same range of hormones as those of normal men."[4] The same is true for women. Analytic theories account for homosexuality on the basis of a dominant mother and a passive father. There is enough truth in the theory, writes White, to make us weigh it carefully, but it is not the whole answer. Sexual urges may be stamped into a young person's behavior pattern by the sexual exploitation of an older person. Sexual stimulation has a way of capturing. It is a complicated matter.

We want to be compassionate to people who are inwardly tormented by the pain of a twisted sexual choice. No matter how those involved in the Gay Movement—who are notably not gay or happy—propagate homosexuality as a viable lifestyle, it is obvious to anyone that men and women are made to satisfy each other sexually. They fit together naturally. It is God's creative design. Any other sexual satisfaction is either artificial or ugly. The knowledge of this is part of the pain of the homosexual.

What do we say, then, to the young man who listens to what the Bible says about homosexual practice and then asks, "You mean God wants me to go through life unfulfilled?" (The New Testament clearly speaks against homosexual practice in both Romans 1 and 1 Corinthians 6.)

We say, "No, God does not mean for you to be unfulfilled. But His way of fulfilling people is different than what you are saying you want to do. His way of fulfilling people is far beyond sexual experience and satisfies the total person."

What we need to hear is that God is the Lord of our sexual urges if we want him to be. Sex is only one part of life. Why make it the whole of life? There may be pain in chastity, but if that is so, people with homosexual feelings are not the only ones who bear pain. Many with heterosexual feelings never marry and choose to remain chaste. Sometimes within marriage the physical condition of one eliminates sexual activity. Pain is one of life's certainties. On the other hand, people do not die from a lack of sex.

Homosexual practice is not an option for anyone who wants to obey God. Increasingly there is scientific evidence to prove it an unwise option for anyone. What is a person to do who is already hooked on this kind of sexual expression? You must want to quit. Don't fool yourself. You *can* stop doing it. You may not be able to immediately control all your thoughts, but you can control your actions. It is painful, perhaps, but that is what the consolation of God is all about. It is stressful, maybe, but that is what God's strength is for.

Second, stay away from temptation. Flee from compromising situations. Find a mature Christian friend, a prayer partner, or a counselor—someone with whom you can be perfectly open. Your practice of homosexuality must stop. If it has never begun, don't allow it to start.

Homosexuality is complex, and we would be naïve to think these brief paragraphs are a complete statement about it. We recommend John White's *Eros Defiled* for a more thorough discussion. While his chapter on homosexuality is compassionate, it bears the title "Two Halves Do Not Make One Whole." This is a telling statement.

Let us repeat: Sexual feelings come from the inside and are a clue to truths about our self-view and our ability to relate to others. They are clues to truths we need to know and evaluate.

## Twisting heterosexuality

This is perhaps the most common twist. It is the male-animal concept. Do what comes naturally; exploit each other; that is what sex is for; put a notch in your belt or paint a rose on the boudoir mirror for every new conquest; sex is something one practices, like gymnastics, so you can get good at it. People think that if they are highly-sexed, they should win a prize. Yet all their promiscuity reveals is great personal insecurity and lack of responsibility.

All sorts of strange sexual behavior that is heterosexual is terribly wrong. Adultery is surely one of these. It is an extreme betrayal of trust. After two people have pledged their trust to each other in marriage, adultery breaks that trust. Suddenly the security of belonging to another is betrayed, and life is never quite safe again. You can't treat someone who is made in the image of God like that.

Sex without marriage is in the same category. You don't waltz into the sanctuary of another person's very being and desecrate that person's wholeness, for sex outside of marriage is a fractured experience.

Other twisted expressions of heterosexuality are seen in the failure to mature in male-female relationships: Obsession with pornography, peep shows, flagellation, bondage, or any other sadistic expression of sex is immature and inappropriate behavior for those made in the image of God. Child-molesting is even more serious. Jesus said strong words about causing children to sin; it would be better for any such person "to have a large millstone hung around his neck and to be drowned in the depths of the sea" (Matthew 18:6). People in the grip of these things deny the seriousness of what they are doing. If any of these are part of your life, seek the help of a Christian counselor immediately.

Living in a world of sexual fantasy is like being in limbo instead of growing up. It is yet another twist in heterosexual feelings. Fantasy is no substitute for genuine relationships. It is a lonely, unhealthy life. Only a commitment to guard one's thoughts and work on what is real and true will pull a person back into the mainstream of life. People have got to want to relate to real people more than their fantasies.

Just because people are heterosexual in feelings and desires—whether married or unmarried—doesn't mean they are handling their sexuality. Lust is a consuming malady wherever it is found, and it shows up in strange ways. An uptight attitude about sexuality (fear of touching, undressing in the closet, finding sexual allusions where none were intended, for example) is also a failure to handle sexuality with the joy and freedom the gift warrants. Sometimes the people who gossip most about sexual behavior are obsessed with sexual thoughts and need as much help as the transgressors. Jesus said a good deal about what we should spend time thinking about.

Falling short of what God has in mind for our sexuality is to *fall short*. We don't have gradations of falling short. Paul wrote to Corinthian Christians: "Do not be deceived: Neither the sexually immoral nor idolators nor adulterers nor male prostitutes nor homosexual offenders nor thieves nor the greedy nor drunkards nor slanderers nor swindlers will inherit the kingdom of God. And that is what some of you were. But you were washed, you were sanctified, you were justified in the name of the Lord Jesus Christ and by the Spirit of our God" (1 Corinthians 6:9–11).

The use of the past tense (*you were*) is a strong statement that things that are wrong can be forgiven and made right by

God's grace. And where would any of us be if that were not so?

Whatever the problem, focusing on the temptation is not the solution because of its strong appeal. In a contest between the feelings and the will, the feelings almost always win. The best of intentions and beliefs can change under the pressure of emotional need. What is needed is what Oswald Chambers called "the expulsive power of a positive new affection." Getting caught up in something larger, focusing away from the temptation to a higher calling, gaining a new view of the love and grace of God—these are more freeing than any human prohibitions.

## Cultural Stress

Satan lies by telling us that he is the one who knows about sex, that he can tell us all about it. But sex is God's idea. He has rooted sexuality into our very being, and because he has made us this way, sexuality is meant for our good. He alone can make sense out of the sexual feelings that were tainted by the Fall. He is not embarrassed when we discuss this with him. We can avoid the pain of experimentation by listening to him; we can receive the freedom of forgiveness by coming to him. Sexuality is both a powerful and a creative force to enrich us in the relationships God has made for us.

Our sexuality needs the continued washing of forgiveness. It is easy, even within marriage, to be selfish about our emotional needs. Our sexuality is not for private abuses, but for enhancing our relationships. As sin has influenced cultural change in the area of male-female relationships, the differences between men and women have resulted in prejudice and competition instead of the complementary partnership intended by God. A spirit of one-upmanship stalks the world in which men try to dominate women, while women try to outwit men. By isolating Bible texts out of context over the years, a group of theologians unwittingly developed teachings that essentially rendered woman an inferior being. This is a sinful attitude that began when Lamech took two wives. Each generation of biblical interpreters reads the works of previous generations and builds interpretations on what has gone before. Partly because this issue did not seem a problem to male theologians, there has been little new research. Only recently have challenges begun to sensitize scholarship.

This has resulted in a strict consignment of roles that, when secularized, portrays woman as body and function rather than gifted and whole as God originally intended. Now we are afloat in a culturally-tainted sea of ideas—with religious domination/ submission on the far right and secular domination/ submission on the far left. Both have the same problem, although the manifestations of each *seems* different on the surface. Men and women today need to think through the creation ideal, and without dismissing all forms of structure from society, examine what kind of partnership would best enrich marriages, churches, and corporate structures in the best stewardship of man and woman created in the image of God. That so few people respect this model reflects the insecurities within us and our need for forgiveness.

Sexual exploitation in any form must be curbed. Our discussion about twisted sex didn't include its weblike reach into society as a whole. Increasingly, barriers against premarital sex are crumbling and are almost leveled to the ground in some parts of the country. The grand plot to get rid of every trace of the shackles of the "Victorian" is aided by contemporary literature, movies, and talk shows where no subject is barred from discussion. A return to the "natural" has been idealized and includes far more than health foods and natural fibers in clothing. "Naturalness" has come to mean nudity and instinctive sexual expression to some, as if there were no standards, no shame, and no meaning in behavior. As a result an estimated twelve million young Americans have sexual diseases. Statistics about teenage abortions, illegitimate children, and single parent families are staggering. This is *freedom*? That blatant pornography—which deadens the senses—is defended on the basis of freedom of the press only shows our confusion.

In a pluralistic society many competing ideologies seem attractive and even logical to those who have no regard for God. Yet quite apart from a convincing theology and Christian ethic, sociologists and historians are issuing warnings about uncurbed sexual expression, and they have been doing so for years. Sigmund Freud in *Civilization and Its Discontents* wrote that civilization is built on the renunciation of instinctual gratification, and that restrictions on sexual life are among the reinforcements a culture needs to progress. An interesting study was done by Cambridge University sociologist J. D. Unwin in 1934. He set out to test Freud's hypothesis that the advance of civilization is correlated with sexual repression and published his findings in *Sex and Culture*. His reasoning is based on respect for society's needs rather than on personhood or God's standards. He came to the conclusion, however, that Freud was right, that the energy necessary for producing what we call civilization is generated by imposing restraints on sexual behavior.[5]

Throughout his later writings, noted historian Arnold J. Toynbee makes an almost evangelistic plea for some kind of return to faith and control of standards for the sake of civilization, although his own faith appears somewhat nebulous.

This secular concern is seldom noted or quoted, even by people who worship at the shrine of sociological and historical research. Harvard sociologist Pitirim Sorokin, wrote, "Increasing heterogeneity, and an antagonism of the imperative-attribute (*oughtness*) and imperative convictions (*commitment*) of the members of society means the shattering, breaking and disintegrating of its network of social relationships. . . . It is like a torn spider web and, like such a broken web, it ceases to control innerly the conduct and relationships of the members of the society. They become 'free,' they lose the clear 'signposts' and guides, showing them what they should do. . . . Their conduct becomes like traffic in a city square with many corners, where no indication is given as to which direction cars must take, what is the right of way, and what is the order of entering and crossing the square. As a result, cars often collide, the air is full of curses . . . traffic is stalled, a general tangle follows."[6]

In their book *The Lessons of History*, the late Will and Ariel Durant wrote, "We frolic in our emancipation from theology, but have we developed a natural ethic—a moral code independent of religion—strong enough to keep our instincts of . . . sex from debasing our civilization into a mire of promiscuity."[7]

The Durants are indifferent to Christianity in that they see it as only one of many religions helpful to mankind and almost resist the conclusions to which their observations drive them. Yet they hope that sexual license may cure itself through its own excess and that our unmoored children may live to see order and modesty become fashionable with clothing more stimulating than nudity.[8] Another statement they make supports our understanding of the importance of careful discipline of our sexuality: "A youth boiling with hormones will wonder why he should not give full freedom to his sexual desires; and if he is unchecked . . . he may ruin his life before he matures sufficiently to understand that sex is a river of fire that must be banked and cooled by a hundred restraints if it is not to consume in chaos both the individual and the group."[9]

Contemporary men and women ignore their own prophets, perhaps because those prophets only observe history rather than proclaim a message that they *know* in their hearts makes sense and undergirds humanity. God, who made us, knows what brings about our good. Sociologists and historians can only observe that this is so, and *that* after the fact.

Chastity makes sense! It makes sense intellectually and emotionally. Chastity is not a thin-lipped, ice-in-the-veins mentality; rather, it is a rule of life that enables a person to live out God's purpose for his sexual existence. It is a holy vitality that expresses itself in liberty toward the other sex, a liberty that has respect and reverence for the other person and for oneself. It has been defined as the very sensuality or affectionate vitality that comes out of a pure heart. Chastity is not a renunciation of pleasure; instead, it is an insurance of true pleasure, a decision based on good theology.

In summary, it is vital that we learn integrity in our sexual lives, especially in the face of the dishonesties of our culture. (Adam was the first of many to blame his problems on his sexuality.) Our integrity will be evident in the way we handle our appetites, our self-discipline, and our interpersonal relationships. It will be seen by a joyful acceptance of being sexual and a concern to express this in ways beneficial to the individual and all of those around us.

---

[1] Lewis Smedes, *Sex for Christians* (Grand Rapids: Wm. B. Eerdmans Publishing Co., 1976), 33.

[2] Ibid., 81.

[3] C. S. Lewis, *God in the Dock: Essays on Theology and Ethics* (Grand Rapids, Wm. B. Eerdmans Publishing Co., 1970), 317.

[4] John White, *Eros Defiled* (Downers Grove, Ill.: InterVarsity Press, 1977), 105. We recommend reading chapter 6, "Two Halves Do Not Make One Whole," if you are interested in more information about homosexuality. Dr. White is a psychiatrist who is first a Christian. He is practical, biblical, and readable.

[5] J. D. Unwin, *Hopousia: The Sexual and Economic Foundations of a New Society*, introduction by Aldous Huxley (New York: Oskar Piest, 1940), 16, 17.

[6] Pitirim A. Sorokin, *Social and Cultural Dynamics* (New York: American Book Co., 1937), 2:597–98. Italics ours.

[7] Will and Ariel Durant, *The Lessons of History* (New York: Simon and Schuster, 1968), 96.

[8] Ibid., 42.

[9] Ibid., 36.

*chapter* 5

# Friendship

A friend sent us a card that read

When someone cares
    it is easier to speak,
    it is easier to listen,
    it is easier to play,
    it is easier to work.
When someone cares
    it is easier to laugh.[1]

We have found it so. It is part of the wonderful things love can do.

The world has too many lonely people. A nationwide survey of 30,000 people of all social and economic classes found that one out of every four Americans suffers from loneliness. The loneliest of these are under twenty-five years of age, and men are lonelier than women.[2]

The personal classified ads in some of our newspapers are a fascinating but painful index of our society. Lonely people try to meet each other through ads by describing themselves as handsome, warm, sensuous, brilliant, earthy, cultured, well-traveled, striking, and fun-loving. These are not unmarried school teachers in Barrow, Alaska, or pipeline workers in the tundra or housewives in the boondocks—they are people who live in Manhattan, Los Angeles, Toronto, Chicago, Ann Arbor, and Berkeley. They are college professors, graduate students, business executives, editors, lawyers, artists, and all of them are saying, "Loneliness is awful."

Tragically, these lonely people often live next door to each other but never reach out. They have illusions that some unknown, unfound person can offer them what a known person cannot. Many of them have sexual encounter in mind, believing it solves loneliness. They seek romantic infatuation but not relationship. Friendship may be the farthest thing from their minds; it is perhaps the most underrated relationship in our society.

### What Is Loneliness?

Loneliness is different from solitude. Solitude is usually chosen, a chance to be alone, to have space for yourself, to think your own thoughts. Aloneness, rightly structured, is restorative and refreshing.

Loneliness is not chosen; it is often depressing, frightening, and debilitating. It is a feeling of emptiness, longing, and actual pain. It feels as if no one cares and has a haunting quality of abandonment. People whose parents were divorced are lonelier as adults than other people, as if there were a lingering feeling of desertion. The loneliness of so many under twenty-five years of age says something about family life, our noisy society, and our culture's substitutes for real life. It is interesting that watching television for extended periods of time prolongs and deepens feelings of loneliness according to the Rubenstein-Shaver survey already cited. Lonely feelings seem to cause a kind of paralysis that keeps a person from solving the problem.

Loneliness is like hunger: "Just as hunger signals the body's need for nourishment, loneliness warns us that important psychological needs are going unmet. Loneliness is a healthy hunger for *intimacy* and *community*—a natural sign that we are lacking companionship, closeness and a meaningful place in the world."[3] Food, alcohol, drugs, soap operas, and frivolity cannot fill the void. They only lead into further uncertainty and confusion.

Intense loneliness is often a result of some sort of change—the loss of someone dear, a move to a new locale, a start at a new job, a first step inside a new school. Change is difficult. If you move away from your roots, you need a whole new set of relationships outside the family. One of our friends described her adjustment to a new city as a year of mourning. Widespread mobility, a high divorce rate, impersonal and crime-ridden cities, the substitution of television and movies for real life, computers that take the place of people, changes brought on by divorce or widowhood or retirement, changes from becoming a mother whose identity is now linked to a small child—no wonder loneliness is rampant.

Loneliness has many guises: "The bittersweet loneliness of adolescence, the desperate loneliness behind swizzle sticks on a Caribbean cruise at Christmas, the masked loneliness of the frantically busy, the collapsed loneliness of the compulsive TV watcher consuming junk food."[4]

Others feel lonely in their marriage when they live together without friendship, as if there were nothing to talk about. Children grow up without ever being friends with their parents. The loss of potentially rich but undervalued relationships is cause for sorrow. A true friend, inside or outside the family, is the best antidote for loneliness. Everyone needs a friend whether he knows it or not.

Our society has thought very little about the value of friendship. Instead, we enlarge the material aspect of life way out of proportion so that both our priorities and our values are out of tune with the way we were made. Friendship has a spiritual quality that scares the materialist. Our technological world has made people mechanical and faceless, and the average man-on-the-street believes that the hidden life is the best life. "What someone doesn't know about you can never be used against you." Ask any success-oriented person about his or her friendships, and you will get a glimpse of attempted autonomy.

Late in life, after living the American dream of amassing wealth beyond the imagination of most men, John D. Rockefeller reflected about his accomplishments and possessions. Asked for his opinions about success, he gave no financial tips except to speak of frugality. Instead he talked about friendship; he treasured above all else, without exception, the value of a *true friend*. That wisdom disappointed some, but Rockefeller had learned what Solomon meant when he wrote: "Two are better than one . . . : If one falls down, his friend can help him up. But pity the man who falls and has no one to help him up! Also, if two lie down together, they will keep warm. But how can one keep warm alone?" (Ecclesiastes 4:9a, 10–11).

The world has in it a lot of empty, hurting people who have tried to fill their lives with things that have never satisfied them. Maybe people are made to relate meaningfully after all. Suspecting that might be true, college students are talking about friendship now, replacing sex as a leading topic of conversation on campus. This search for intimacy has led some to conclude that sex may be the least intimate thing they do.[5] There has got to be more to life than that. Suddenly, every publishing house has a book on friendship, each one of which says that we have given it too little importance in our culture—as if we had suddenly discovered a shining gem in the clutter of life.

Our grandparents used to say that choosing friends is a serious matter. There is a friendship even among thieves. Men have been known to fail because they have chosen friends unwisely and trusted the wrong people. Women have had their hearts broken for the same reason. How many people have been diverted from the *best* because their friends were content with less. Friends can infect us with poor attitudes, encourage our worst habits, and accompany our descent. If you want to climb upward spiritually, it is best to have friends who are going the same way: "Do two walk together unless they have agreed to do so?" The ideas and ideals of friends are borrowed unconsciously, which makes the old adage true: "We are known by the company we keep."

## Friendship: Respected but Sometimes Suspected

Friendship seems the happiest and most fully human of all loves according to C. S. Lewis in *The Four Loves*. Although this observation takes us by surprise, it is worth pondering. We have not thought of friendship in that way in our culture. Instead of valuing friendship, Lewis says, it has been the least important of our relationships because "it has the least commerce with our nerves; there is nothing throaty about it; nothing that quickens the pulse or turns you red or pale."[6] Friendship has no romance.

Besides that, it puts you out of step with the pack. The community may even dislike and distrust friendship, and its leaders often do. Something about those little knots of friends makes heads of companies, schools, churches, and other institutions feel uneasy. We choose our friends, and that very selectivity makes friendship seem undemocratic. Friendship withdraws people from the masses by twos or threes, so that to say, "These people are my friends" implies that others are not,[7] which seems to show favoritism.

But the very freedom of friendship is what makes it so special, for no friendship had to be. You go along, unaware that the other person exists. The other person also goes along unaware of your existence until one day you meet and something clicks. You feel understood, and you sense a richness in the other person that calls for exploration, spontaneity, joy, fun. Indeed the words *friend* and *free* are related. The Old English word *freo* means free, not in bondage, noble, glad. The Old English word *freon* means to love, and the word *freoud* becomes our modern English word *friend*. A friend allows others to be themselves, to think their own thoughts, to own their own feelings.

Friendship makes dictators and authoritarians uneasy because it resists the herd instinct; it is for free spirits who laugh together. It sets up its own agenda, unknown to anyone else—and that can be threatening.

Perhaps it is this uneasiness that leads people to wonder if a close friendship between two people of the same sex is likely to be a homosexual relationship. Whispers about such possibilities have probably scared more people away from intimacy and wholesome friendship than we can ever surmise. Lewis says that those who whisper such nonsense betray that they have never had a friend.

Jonathan's and David's poignant friendship has not escaped the notice of the cynics in this regard. The language of Scripture is strong: "Jonathan became one in spirit with David, and he loved him [David] as himself" (1 Samuel 18:1); David sings of his love for the slain Jonathan: "Your love for me was wonderful, more wonderful than that of women" (2 Samuel 1:26). Their exemplary friendship involved commitment (the making of a covenant), true love (Jonathan looked beyond the bold truth that David was a usurper of Jonathan's own right to the throne), and *loyalty* and *trustworthiness* in the face of great danger. David's commitment lead him to care for Jonathan's offspring long after Jonathan had been slain. Somehow their friendship rose above the political intrigue of King Saul's court and was probably the closest relationship either of them ever had.

The Apostle Paul had a similar relationship with Timothy. We cover over their friendship with a "father-son" label, but friendships are not hindered by age. Paul writes to Timothy, "Recalling your tears, I long to see you, so that I may be filled with joy" (2 Timothy 1:4) and "Do your best to come to me quickly" (2 Timothy 4:9). Even Jesus drew three of the twelve disciples into a more intimate relationship with himself. The Bible seems to call people to risk-taking friendships and exhorts us to love others as we love ourselves.

In a similar way, friendships between men and women are questioned and almost always made into romances as though such friendships could not possibly be wholesome, holy, and practical. What does it mean to have brothers and sisters in Christ? Are brothers and sisters remote from each other, unfriendly, and superficial in their encounters? And what of Jesus love for Martha and Mary? Did Paul have a special friendship with Priscilla, even though she was married to Aquila? Or do we simply consign that to another culture?

Married people can and do have friendships with others not of the same gender with a glad wholesomeness that includes the marriage partner in the friendship. When you can prattle on about another friend with your spouse with complete transparency, then the doors of friendship are open and trustworthy. If, however, any hint of jealousy, insecurity, or exclusiveness threatens the marriage because of such a friendship, then loyalty insists that the primary relationship needs care and nurture. We are given our heads so we can use them as well as our hearts. It takes healthy people to carry off a friendship of any kind.

The possibility of sexual temptation exists in any relationship. Friendship has no corner on this. Sexual sin makes up the plot of a thousand broken marriages and other sordid stories. But as Martin Marty writes in his book called *Friendship*,[8] there *are* safeguards against transgression among people of will who prize honor and fidelity, which we see in tens of millions of unbroken marriages and unsoiled friendships. To deny friendship based on this fear would be folly and would "overendow sex with meaning and terror" that it does not *need* to have.

Jesus was a realist when he said the very inclination to sexual sin should be handled ruthlessly in a person's heart. He said adultery is not just physical disloyalty; it is also "lusting in your heart," and he said, "If your right eye causes you to sin, gouge it out." Be honest, he said, about what it means to be pure. Instead, people discuss "how far they can go" in relationships and entertain the idea of impurity. Inappropriate jokes and suggestive remarks foul the air of today's marketplace. This misses the whole point of the strength of Jesus' teaching. Even ministers make what are supposed to be amusing remarks for comic relief in their sermons and make innuendos about innocent events ("Don't let my wife know about this. Ha. Ha."). If we toy around with any ideas like this, even in jest, we have already bought into this world's system that includes adultery, according to Jesus' teaching. Maybe we wouldn't be so afraid of our relationships if our commitment to holiness was greater.

Christians must make a commitment to faithfulness and to purity. We have been psychologized into a sliding standard based on our own urges. A commitment to holiness means there are some things I *will not do*; there are some thoughts I *will not entertain*. Fidelity is not negative, however; *it is commitment to something higher*. We need to hear a call to this kind of commitment. Remember, temptation usually comes in by a door left deliberately open.

All our relationships need the safeguard of proper commitment and proper setting. Honesty is crucial. No matter how conditioned we may be by liberalized standards of sexual behavior, every one knows when that proper commitment is in danger of being violated. That is why we have emphasized that being made in God's image means we are capable and responsible for choice; we have a will and can choose what is good.

God has made us for relationships, and friendship is at its best when two people are joined by a third or a fourth, if they be kindred souls. "To divide is not to take away" in friendship; more participants enrich it. The problem is more often the scarcity of kindred souls. Nonetheless, friendship is an open alliance. It is the least jealous of the four kinds of loves, says Lewis.[9] There is something sick about a friendship that makes other people outsiders and feel inferior or disdained. Friendship is a prize, and the enemy, who steals good things, knows it.

## Defining Friendship

What is this thing called friendship? We get mixed up because we use the word to cover almost anyone we recognize. One time, while visiting an old acquaintance, we noticed that the conversation was taking a mind-boggling turn. He turned every subject we talked about into stories of the celebrities who were friends of his. He would say, "Do you know Joe Petrie?" Yes, we had heard of him. "Well, he's a friend of mine." It got us thinking about the use of the word *friend*. After all, a man can only have so many friends, if we define the relationship correctly. What he really meant was that he had met these people, conversed with them, and would call them by name if he saw them again. To have too many friends is to devalue friendship; careless use of the word depletes its meaning.

It is easy to call colleagues "friends." You see them often, sometimes every day. You have a common work that gives you a common vocabulary and a common concern. And that commonality can be mistaken for the commitment of friendship. Obviously, it can be the beginning of a friendship, since friendships are built on common interests, but unless it goes further, it doesn't qualify. The problem with mistaking colleagues for friends is in the hurt of discovering that they do not have the loyalty required of friendship and that any depth of understanding is missing.

A friendly acquaintance is some one you chat with about

politics, according to Adelaide Bry. Casual friends are people you argue with about politics, but true-blue friends, to use her phrase, don't talk about politics. They have more important things to talk about.[10]

It is a bit like talking about the weather with our closest friend. Instead, we get past that subject in a hurry and talk about ideas and feelings—the kind of sharing we anticipate so eagerly in being together. Superficial friends share one or two common interests, says Montaigne in his essay "On Friendship," but between friends there is a deep, abiding commitment that is spiritual and enhancing to both.

Americans seem to have a habit of making superficial, social "friendships," if they can be called that. We tend to speak of friends and are hardly known to anyone. In contrast, it is common for Europeans and Asians to treat people only as acquaintances until some depth of communication has been tested and established. We received a letter from a German colleague telling us that after spending time with the village doctor for over a year, they had discussed being friends and moved to a first-name basis. They made a commitment to be friends. In contrast, we had been with the doctor whenever we visited overseas and had assumed an easy camaraderie with him. We called him by his first name almost immediately. It was superficial, warm, embracing— and very American.

Obviously there are levels of knowing another person. This can be illustrated by the following diagram. Each arrow represents a person in one's life. The height to which the arrow rises represents the intensity of the relationship. The deep commitment of friendship only exists with those few at the top of the graph, and only one goes to the very peak. Usually that is a pattern in the exceptional marriage.

**Intensity of Friendships**

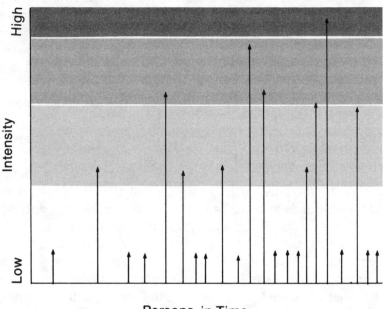

Persons, in Time

The bottom line of the graph could also be a time line. It pictures how many superficial friendships occur early in life, and how with maturity the ability to make deep friendships increases.

C. S. Lewis says a friendship begins when someone says, "What? You too? I thought I was the only one."[11] It is a matter of seeing the same truth, of caring about the same truth. The focus is not on the friendship, but on the ideas shared. In other words, saying "I want a friend" is not the secret to friendship, but rather, exploring whether there is anything to be a friend about is a better beginning. One does not make friends; one finds them.

Genuine friendship has so many facets that it seems to be an idea for the philosophers. Yet friendship as an idea is different from thinking of a particular person who is your friend, which involves the heart. When we read the observations of others on friendship, think of a friend, and say, "Yes, that's also true." Martin Marty says that "friendship is a gift of God for his sorrowing creatures to give them joy worthy of their destiny." He quotes Richard Rolle (1349) who said, "Holy friendship truly is from God, that amid the wretchedness of this exile, we be comforted with the counsel of friends until we come to Him." It is good to experience the depth of those concepts—comfort and joy.

Marty writes that like the grace of God itself, the gift of friendship in our lives is like the the bass line in music; it gives a grounding while the treble can fret and trill. It is part of the firm ground on which we can walk, so firm that we can dance without reflecting on it. . . . When friendship disappears we suddenly become conscious of what it meant to us—as if the bass notes were gone and we had only aimless and unharmonious notes left, as if the ground had dropped from beneath us. Without friends, we become more self-occupied and busy with the tasks of survival and relocating our identity.[12]

Ranier Maria Rilke spoke of "two solitudes [who] protect and touch and greet each other." He penned those words in praise of love, but it describes friendship as well. When we think of friendship, words like *loyalty*, *trust*, *acceptance*, *love*, *understanding*, and *support* come to mind. That kind of friendship takes commitment. It is not, "I'll go with you unless someone better asks me." Rather, it is the kind of commitment that lead our grandmothers to sign their letters, "Your devoted friend," as Pamela Reeve says (in her booklet *Relationships*), while she signs hers "Love, Pam." "Love" is an expression of warmth and feeling, she says, but with no strings attached. "Devoted friend" adds the commitment of the will.[13]

## Friendship Isn't Easy

Friendship is costly. When you have a friend you lose some liberty—the liberty of no accountability, the liberty of no interruptions. Friends need to talk to each other; their hearts reach out; and that can make them troublesome. Friends get sick and need help. They sometimes die. You have to get involved to be a friend. You have to take time to maintain a relationship, and maintaining a relationship also means forgiving since all of us are fallen. It means bearing with one another. "I will not desert you." That is all part of loyalty.

*Loyalty.* Loyalty means that you will always be for me—not for my wrongs—but *for me.* I can count on you to believe the best about me, to stand in my shoes, to communicate truth to me. Loyalty has a strong note of truth rather than pretense. I can accept positive praise or critical exhortation. With eyes wide open we commit ourselves to friendship. (It is this combination of loyalty and reality that keeps us from fooling ourselves about questionable relationships and inappropriate sexual responses. It keeps us from using people.)

We are loyal to our friend, but we need also to be loyal to the commitment of friendship. Friendships are sometimes blown apart when one member forgets that commitment. A friendship that is as close as a brother-sister relationship, for example, will blossom until one person is suddenly overcome with romantic feelings. Naturally, friendships among unattached, single people often move into romantic love and marriage, but that change in relationship must happen within both people. Commitment to friendship may some-times mean foregoing feelings of love and patiently waiting for God to make known his plan. Sometimes loyalty endures the terrible test of a friend choosing romantic interest in another person.

We can conjure up all kinds of real-life situations in which this fragile thing called friendship may encounter the snares of strange feelings. Some are appropriate and some are grossly inappropriate. What does one do? Loyalty and commitment to friendship act as a ballast in the turbulent sea of emotion, and most often one is called to love *more* rather than less.

*Trust.* Trust is crucial to friendship. You could share many good ideas to stimulate me, but unless I feel safe, I cannot draw you to me as a friend. Friends have to keep confidences. You will not betray me. You will do me good, not evil. You will tell me no lies and give no false or broken promises. There will be no talking about me to others in a way that will demean me. You will not take what you know about me and use it against me. Friendship is a dialogue between two trusting people. You cannot be creative in your communica-tion if you think the other person is going to stab you in the back.

The glory of friendship, wrote Ralph Waldo Emerson, is not the outstretched hand, nor the kindly smile, nor the joy of companionship—treasured as these may be. Its glory is the spiritual inspiration that comes with the discovery that someone else believes in and trusts me.

*Loving acceptance.* Feelings need to be expressed in a good friendship. Human warmth, expressions of love and affection, touching, hugs, small favors, keepsakes, surprises—friends find so many ways to say "I like you." We need reassurance. A friend is someone who understands your heart, who knows you, and in whose life you feel welcome.

It is safe to be yourself with a friend because you don't have to earn acceptance. You can express who you are and say whatever feelings or thoughts come to mind. With acquaintances you tend to edit yourself to fit their slightly unreal image of you. Not so with a friend. You can be with a person for an afternoon or three hours and find a friendship beginning. Another person will remain only an acquaintance after thirty years. (It is regrettable that some marriage partners stay only acquaintances.)

Friends sometimes move thousands of miles away, and life changes. Friendships become less intense, less involved. It is hard to keep in touch. But let those friends meet again after long separation, and the spark is still there. Friends usually take up right where they left off. Sometimes it begins as if they are completing the last sentence they said to each other. At other times, meeting again has all the warm comfortableness that makes catching up easy; it goes directly to the heart of the matter with no small talk. A friend not heard from recently sends a cartoon or a brief note that speaks so appropriately to the situation. He knows, he remembers, and it is like a warm surprise. The phone rings and after the flurry of "It's been so long!" two people share their hearts with the safety that has always been there.

When friends are together the barometer of the heart registers pleasure, comfort, stimulation, new ideas, relaxation, laughter. A good friendship is a deep human need. It provides the accepting climate for us to become what God wants us to be.

"Oh, the comfort, the inexpressible comfort of feeling safe with a person, having neither to weigh thoughts nor measure words, but to pour them all out together—wheat and chaff— knowing that a faithful hand will keep the wheat and, with a breath of kindness, blow the chaff away." That quotation, attributed to a variety of sources, captures the essence of loving acceptance.

Acceptance need not and must not always mean perfect agreement. "As iron sharpens iron, so one man sharpens another" (Proverbs 27:17). Our ideas are straightened out and clarified—and some of them happily discarded—as a result of the give-and-take of the intellectual dimension of friendship. The virtues of friendship presume an intellectual content. Friendship is not a mushy, sentimental feeling devoid of substance. It is thinking together, thrashing out ideas and insights in the context of acceptance.

IIS magazine carried a filler item that read, "Sometimes grindstone polish comes in peopled forms for smoothing jointed noses and waxing cold hearts to love's shine." Those who have felt the honing of genuine friendship would say, "Amen." Each of us has friendships like that, the kind of relationship that makes you say, "She makes me a better person," or "He stimulates me to my best thinking."

*Understanding* and *Supportiveness*. To understand and support does not mean that friends become counselors. Dependency, dominance, and overinvolvement hurt friendships. There are some things friends cannot do for each other, and they need to talk about these. Friends can only be friends; in fact, they are best at being friends, not counselors. Counselors and therapists are professional roles.

Having said that, it does not follow that friends do not support one another in face of problems, offer suggestions, prayer, and help. Having friends does not mean we avoid conflict, but rather that we have support in learning how to handle it. "Talking things over" with a friend is one of the most useful parts of friendship. Friends will *feel* with you and that takes away the loneliness. They widen your world, give perspective, and suggest options. Mostly friends just listen, and that is their best gift. Is there anything more nourishing than a quiet walk in the woods with a friend?

Pamela Reeve writes about structuring a relationship by defining what the limits are, what the responsibilities of each are, what the expectations are so there will be less disappointment. Sometimes roles need definitions; a person may need to say, for example, "No, I cannot be your mother, but I will be your friend." Structuring makes it easier to talk about abuses, forgiveness, and the tendency of one to control the other. Often the controlling member is the one with the problem.

When that kind of structuring is necessary, the situation is almost always a counseling relationship in which the self-giving rests heavily on one person. It lacks the mutuality that makes genuine friendship such a pleasure. Generally, a friend has a keen instinct for the need of the other person, which is what makes the friendship what it is. However, some relationships are on their way to becoming friendships and may need the discipline of such rules. Quality friendships often develop out of painful struggle to communicate as well as understand oneself and the other person. The more intimate the relationship, the more monitoring it requires. Marriage is a good example.

Sometimes friendship is tested by a spirit of competition. That always hurts. If a person dies a little when someone else succeeds or finds it difficult to be glad when another prospers, we question if this is genuine friendship. We expect that of enemies, but of friends? One of our delights is the way in which friends respond with overwhelming gladness whenever something good happens to us. In fact, they help make it happen. Jealousy and envy have deep roots in the human heart, and unless these poisons are honestly purged, any relationship is in trouble. Feelings of negative emotions are sneaky, but a true friend will admit the problem because talking about it usually leads to a solution. That is true for friendships, marriages, and families.

## Friendship, Overprogramming, and Underplanning

A busy life is a barrier against closeness. As we were walking down a rural lane with a couple who have been our friends for many years, they told us of their need to develop close friendships. Now that their children are grown and no longer at home, he is putting more time into his business, and she is going to school and working part time. Some of her classes are at night. They manage to keep touch with each other and caught up on household responsibilities, but time runs out for friendships.

A young couple we know told us of the husband's heavy travel schedule and their time-consuming involvement with raising three young children. He is gone too much, and she is too busy with the children. A single-career person bemoans job pressures and part-time grad-school commitments that leave only time for keeping life together. An overly busy lifestyle is an enemy to friendship. Friendships demand the leisure of talk, play, and what efficient people call "wasting time." Friends by their very existence are a judgment on the overprogrammed life, writes Marty. We cut out such inefficiencies as friendship when we need to cherish them.[14]

Happiness *is* being married to your best friend. Being a lover and a friend are not mutually exclusive. (C. S. Lewis said that lovers usually stand face to face, absorbed in each other, while friends stand side by side, absorbed in a common interest.[15] A combination of both makes a wonderful marriage.) Married people run the risk of being satisfied with the dimensions of their life together and make no effort for outside friendships. Married people need friends—his friends, her friends, and their friends. Friends widen the married person's world, give needed perspective, and provide a variety of interests. Being married does color friendship ("Wedding bells are breaking up that old gang of mine!"), but two people who are completely wrapped up in each other makes a small world. No person can possibly meet all the needs of another; it puts an unbearable strain on the relationship. Rarely do a husband and wife find kindred spirits in another couple, but it is a worthy goal. More often it takes more than one other unit to meet the friendship needs of a married couple.

Some argue that men only use friendship as stepping stones for success, that their idea of a friendship is a business lunch or a social gathering that gives them connections. But those are contacts, not friendships. As more and more women move into positions of power in the marketplace, will this mark their lives also? Will using people become a wholesale substitute for nurturing friendships?

Although it may be an overgeneralization, men seem to shy away from emotional intimacy and handle relationships with others on the level of camaraderie or companionship. A golf partner or a fishing buddy do not necessarily make a friendship. Men who do not take easily to intimacy often fall into two categories. The first enters marriage while very young, never having learned tenderness or how to communicate deep feelings. He considers intimacy a sign of weakness and cannot rely emotionally on others even in times of stress. He doesn't know how. When the bottom falls out, he has no resources. He may begin to drink or hide from people, but he does not confide. We have often commented on men in our acquaintance, "I wonder if he has any friends. Does anyone know him well enough to help him?"

The second type of evading male needs support but doesn't trust anyone enough to ask for it, probably because of some painful rejection in his past. He knows he needs help, but he erects barriers by being vulgar, rude, sloppy, or otherwise uncomely. He sets up further rejection based on his behavior, as if to say, "I know you can't meet my needs anyway." If anyone calls his bluff (and wives are good at this) and gets on the inside, he will accept the love and support they offer.

Female evaders exist, but there are fewer of them. We need an emotional revolution among men that gives them the freedom to be more human in this area, and we think it is coming; indeed, it is already here in the generation of young men who have rejected the corporate model or the scientific role and have entered the humanities in our universities instead. Perhaps that is an unfair generalization because we can think of dozens who break that stereotype. Yet the exceptions tend to be the rule.

The telephone, a mobile lifestyle, and the pace of living have made letter writing almost obsolete. When we do write, our notes seem shallow and event-oriented. (The same applies to recording our thoughts in a journal—which is far different from keeping a diary. In one you write thoughts and feelings; in the other, just the facts.) Our failure to write letters to those at a distance or leave notes for those closer at hand is a great loss to both receiver and sender. Life goes by so quickly that we reflect little on what we have found valuable. We fail to record the development of our thinking and inwardly pass our days in a daze. We say things on paper that we forget to say in person, and we say them differently, more poetically, more meaningfully. That is why a birthday or special-day letter is tucked away as a treasure to nourish the heart again and again.

The pace of our lives makes us almost juvenile in establishing relationships. We feel lonely, and then we find a kindred spirit and delve in too quickly, not pacing or monitoring the development of the friendship. It is like a romantic infatuation. Pamela Reeve tells of rushing home to tell her grandmother about the wonderful, best-ever friend she made in school that day. Her grandmother said, "Dear, you have to summer with her and winter with her and summer with her again. Then tell me about your friend."[16] Friendship *is* based on knowing. Good things can always stand the test of time.

## Changing Friendships

Friendships also change, because we change. Relationships that were once close may move to a different level of commitment because of the variables in a person's life. If a man marries, for example, his friendships change to a different frequency simply because of the intensity of his relationship with a new wife. Friends are a reflection, a mirror of who you are right now. You will find yourself changed by many factors in life. Some friendships may be affected by these changes. Often friends do not even know they are parting; they just gradually go separate ways.

Marty says, "To keep our sanity, we have to remember that even friends are like ships passing in the night; their lights penetrate each other's zones of visibility, their solitudes touch and greet for a while—but then they move on. The mind is not able to register nor the heart capable of storing all the positive contacts we have had through the years. We have to sort, to eliminate, to let go, and let drop."[17]

He likens this to books on his shelf that have had to make room for new ones. Letting friendships fade or die, he says, may be part of a natural passage or a call of God.

We might agree that this happens to our less in-depth relationships, but we doubt that this ever happens to friends with whom we have made meaningful, mature commitments. The chart about the intensity of friendships needs to be referred to again. Situations may change and alter the way the commitment expresses itself, but those deeper commitments of friendship remain.

Patricia Ward deplores our planned impermanence in relationships. She quotes Thomas Griffith, a columnist in *Atlantic* who notes that "impermanence is in our heads." We have internalized impermanence and superficiality in relating and communicating with people. Ward says, "I would argue that viewing life as impermanent makes us relate to people in a way that protects us from being bonded to 'significant others' on a long-term basis. The loss of the sense of bonding between friends is one of the least recognized ways in which chaos and disorder have invaded the fabric of our society. Friendship is viewed less and less as a volitional commitment."[18] It is part of our throw-away society— planned obsolescence.

We are particularly concerned when this expectation of impermanence hits marriage. "Oh, we've drifted apart," he says. "She has outgrown him," another comments. And these are used as excuses for divorce. It can be a convenient way to get out of the responsibility of keeping commitments and refining one's own person.

The commitment of love creates for another person a climate in which that person can become all God wants that one to be. It is no mistake that marriage vows are made before God and a company of witnesses, because marriage is not a private matter; it is the joining of families; it is the creating of family. No human commitment we make is as all-encompassing of our total person as marriage. Friendship is

God's beautiful gift to enrich our days on earth. A good marriage is also a friendship, but the two are not equal commitments.

## Friendship and the Single Life

The number of adult singles in our society is growing. Those figures, in part, reflect the growing ranks of divorced people, but a large proportion are young people who have never married. Some of them deliberately postpone marriage for career reasons, and others desire to find out who they are before linking their life up with someone else (not a bad idea!). Most of them are hopeful about finding the right person and long for the intimacy of the marriage relationship.

But whatever the reason for being unattached, *people do not have to be lonely.* A good friendship offers a nourishing kind of intimacy, a fulfillment that many do not find in marriage. People who can't sustain deep friendships, who are insensitive and have rough edges, will also have trouble sustaining a marriage.

Don't concentrate on romance; concentrate on friendship. It is the all-purpose relationship that everyone needs. Friendship requires what any love relationship does: trust, affection, self-revelation, caring. People who are looking for romance often by-pass those qualities because today's sexual propaganda has such a loud voice. Legitimate urges keep them from questioning whether all the hype is true. Sex is not an adequate basis for anything except sex. Any good relationship demands more, and people who give themselves away too easily find that they are mistaken about what is the pearl of great price.

Not knowing how to handle strong sexual urges complicates the lives of singles. Some men find it easier not to develop intimacy with women because of unresolved sexual feelings. Hiding seems to simplify life. But hiding ignores the wholeness of our humanity. We are whole entities: body, soul, and spirit. In important ways, the body expresses who we are as much as our soul and spirit. We are a unity, and when all parts are in harmony, then our sexual nature is controlled by that harmony. In secular society the body is portrayed as a sex machine. The Christian knows this is not so.

Yielding to premarital sex, whether intercourse or heavy petting, is taking the easy road of physical involvement and evading the difficult encounter of personalities. Couples deceive themselves about the significance of their relationship. In a contest between emotion and intellect, emotion almost always wins and betrays what the mind says is true. Because such activity lacks wholeness, it cannot satisfy.

The Apostle Paul, in writing to the Ephesians, is realistic about the strength and confusion of sexual urges. He says that there should not even be a hint of sexual immorality among believers; in fact, he says, it is not even good to joke about the subject because jesting introduces it into the mind and brings a person closer to doing it (Ephesians 5:3–4). Instead, what strikes us with new force is his advice to give thanks for our sexuality. Thankfulness sees God's hand in making mankind both male and female; it sees sex as a God-given gift. In contrast, vulgarity leads to a warped view of sex. It seems to us that honest thankfulness before God for one's sexuality would lead to *his* creative solutions for the sexual pressure singles often face.

"Living together" is so common today that a discussion of friendship seems like talk from another planet. But maybe a message from another world is exactly what is needed. The physical bonding of two people in sexual intercourse is a psychic bonding as well. Recreational sex leads to fractured personalities. We see so many involved in recreational sex that we mistake it for the norm.

It is said that part of the problem singles face in making good friendships is finding a kindred spirit. But singles sometimes set themselves up for their own disappointments. Young people in particular have difficulty getting past the dormitory mentality regarding roommates, where you are assigned someone and make the best of it. Two women team up for disastrously troubled and lonely apartment living; men do so even more easily. The arrangement has no commitment beyond the rent, and the person is superficially known—until the tension of sharing the same space hits the relationship or school is over.

Why not invest part of the same time and care in finding a compatible friend and roommate as one would in finding a solid marriage partner? That sounds like a large order, but we have given so little priority to friendship that a kind of emotional promiscuity results. We need to think of friendship as commitment. Investing in good friendships brings more happiness than waiting around for The Big Event (marriage) to happen!

While singles wait, they often live shabbily, with "temporary" written over the way they eat, keep their personal belongings, and relate to other people. Sometimes there is an obvious underlying anxiety, and anxious people do not make good friends. Singles need a home to which they can invite people—a place of peace for themselves. It doesn't always have to be shared with a roommate; solitude and loneliness are not the same. Some people want private space, but living alone can give a person rigid habits.

Our great fear for singles, however, is not that they will

never marry, but that they will avoid the kind of in-depth relationships that refine the spirit and enrich the heart. They neglect the human. Something negative happens to the heart if a constant absorption with self deprives us of the relationships for which we were made.

People without family responsibilities are the freest to develop meaningful friendships. They should be the freest to give themselves in service to needy people, to handle organizational responsibilities, to develop new talents, to take a new lesson, or whatever. And it is while we *live* that we grow and find the people we need in our lives. It may take waiting for God to act on our behalf, but the Bible says good things happen to us while we wait, and that kind of waiting has the productive presence of the Holy Spirit in our lives. When genuine, enriching friendship comes, it always has the touch of his presence.

We have two women friends who long ago teamed up vocationally. They share a home, their vacations, and their extensive ministry. Each provides a dimension of personality for their friendship and for the ministry that the other lacks. Their friendship has solid commitment and richness that you would like to see in many marriages. Both of them are such special people that they have had to put up with the usual facetious remarks about "unclaimed blessings" over the years, but that kind of comment only reveals that we have limited meaningful relationships to one category: marriage. And that isn't right.

Older singles—divorced or widowed—have more difficulty in finding a kindred spirit with whom to have genuine friendship for a variety of reasons: they often have a later start in establishing close relationships outside the family; there are complications in their family relationships; there is the distraction of the grieving process; there is sometimes a more fully developed expectation of what the other person must be to satisfy the need. And they often lack the freedom to meet new people. God is not hindered from creative solutions by any of these situations. Asking him and trusting him are the two surest ways to have emotional needs met with quality friendships.

Recently a divorced mother of two children talked about her feelings immediately after her divorce. She said that she did not need, at that time, a man in her life; she needed godly women friends to help her through her trauma and to teach her how to be godly. Now, considerably later, she may well be interested in a more serious friendship with a man, but we can see in her life the peaceful fruit of the decision she made earlier. She rightly understood that the tragedy she faced was her opportunity to review and strengthen her personal life.

Others we have known, and grieved over, have jumped from the frying pan into the fire; they chose another loser-relationship, as if their ego desperately needed assurance. An inability to face life with honesty and a lost sense of personhood seem to spur on this behavior.

We say unequivocally that same-sex friends are the most nourishing relationships in times of trauma. They prevent misunderstandings and poor decisions, which are often based on emotional needs.

Friendships between single men and women—we've often referred to them as brother-sister relationships—can be the enriching ways to know the possibilities of maleness and femaleness. These kinds of friendships are best accomplished in groups—small support groups, athletic-interest groups, Bible study groups, and so on. They are not begun at singles bars or places where people are looking for "someone." It can take the form of group dating and give those involved the freedom to be who they are with no strings attached. It is an opportunity to be known and to know others.

We advocate friendship, the freest kind of relationship. One or two persons can have a deep commitment to friendship, to responsibility for each other. These are the rich people, whether they marry or not.

## Dimensions of Love

We need *love* in our lives. C. S. Lewis had four categories for love based upon the four Greek words translated "love" (*The Four Loves*). The words are *storge* (pronounced "STORE-gay"), *philia*, *eros*, and *agape* (pronounced "ah-GAH-pay"). A brief and incomplete description of these categories shows how we need each one of them.

*Storge* is simply affection, a warm comfortableness, a satisfaction of being together with little required. It is camaraderie and companionship.

*Philia* is the mutual friendship about which we have written in this book. It serves ("He [will] lay down his life for his friends,") and it also receives ("You are my friends if you do what I command" [John 15:13, 14]).

*Eros* is legitimate desire, the state of yearning and hungering for what will satisfy or for what is good, and though it can be applied to sexual desire, it actually means a preoccupation with the beloved's total person.

*Agape* is God's kind of love that gives without the condition that anything be given in return. It is seen throughout the Bible as God's love goes before man's (1 John 4:10) and makes the supreme act of self-giving through Jesus Christ's death for the world's sins (Philippians 2:5-11).

But it is the dimension of *agape* love—self-giving love—

that transforms all other loves. Friendship may be primarily *philia*, but *agape* infuses friendship with an unselfish, unde-manding quality that makes the reciprocal relationship more than a market-type exchange.[19] We can share in this love, imperfect as we are, as God in his grace pours his love into our hearts by the Holy Spirit that he has given to us (Romans 5:5). *Agape* changes the marriage relationship into mutual servanthood; it performs a similar miracle in the church.

Happily we can know something of this unselfish kind of love in our friendships. Otherwise they would be in a constant state of brokenness and offer us very little satisfac-tion. The responsibilities of friendship—commitment, loyal-ty, trust, acceptance, understanding, supportiveness—all require the overlay of God's grace in supplying us with self-giving, serving love. Friendships need the divine protection of *agape* love lest they disintegrate and destroy themselves with earthly selfishness.

In the loneliness of living in a broken world, asking God for a friend is a legitimate prayer request. He longs to meet all our emotional needs, and he alone can help us be a friend. Friendship is a mutual relationship, giving and receiving. Being a friend is often far more difficult than finding one.

Still, in the end, our friendships are often chosen for us. It is not a matter of chance; rather, a secret master of ceremonies has been at work. Christ, who said to his disciples, "You have not chosen me, but I have chosen you," also says to friends, "You have not chosen one another, but I have chosen you for one another." Friendship is not a reward for our discriminating taste, says Lewis, but it is the instrument by which God reveals to each the beauties of all the others. At this feast it is he who has spread the board and it is he who has chosen the guests. It is he who is the host.[20] And we do well to reckon on his presence.

Yet no friendship on earth can truly satisfy our deepest needs. When Bernard of Clairvaux wrote,

> From the best bliss that earth imparts
> We turn unfilled to Thee again,

he grasped the deepest truth about our relational needs. A transaction of grace must occur in which God chooses to bring us to himself and to be our friend in the most profound way. God is a friend beyond all others, who numbers the hairs on our head, who is acquainted with all our ways, who knows us thoroughly, who loves us with an everlasting love, who continues his faithfulness to us, who considered us worth dying for, and who plans to make us new creations in Christ Jesus.

---

[1] The card was designed by Susan Schultz.

[2] Carin Rubenstein and Phillip Shaver, In Search of Intimacy (New York: Delacorte Press, 1982), 3.

[3] Ibid., 3.

[4] Ibid., ii, from the introduction by Gail Sheehy.

[5] Adelaide Bry, Friendship (New York: Grosset and Dunlap, 1979), 14.

[6] C. S. Lewis, The Four Loves (New York: Harcourt, Brace and Co., 1960), 88.

[7] Ibid., 90.

[8] Martin E. Marty, Friendship (Allen, Tex.: Argus Communications, 1980), 184.

[9] Lewis, The Four Loves, 92.

[10] Bry, *Friendship*, 20.

[11] Lewis, *The Four Loves*, 98.

[12] Marty, *Friendship*, 75.

[13] Pamela Reeve, *Relationships* (Portland, Ore.: Multnomah Press, 1982), 7.

[14] Marty, *Friendship*, 181.

[15] Lewis, *The Four Loves*, 91.

[16] Reeve, *Relationships*, 16.

[17] Marty, *Friendship*, 209.

[18] Patricia A. Ward, "The Bond of Love In an Age of Easy Good-Bys," HIS magazine, May 1982, 19.

[19] Ideas taken from a lecture by Arthur Holmes, Professor of Philosophy at Wheaton College, Wheaton, Illinois, in 1979.

[20] Lewis, *The Four Loves*, 126.

*chapter* 6

# Kinship

"A man's family sets him apart from all other living creatures. Who else has children he can call his own for longer than it takes to set them on their feet or on their way? The most loving animals—the vixen, the bear, the lioness— teach their cubs to make their own world, and to forget them; after the eagle has taught her eaglet to fly, she will see him no more. Calf, colt, grasshopper, dragonfly—all go their separate ways as soon as they can. Only man stands with his children from first to last, from birth to death, and to the grave."[1]

Both of us have a keen sense of belonging: We belong to

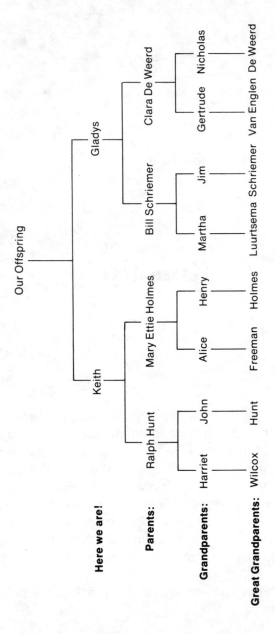

Our Simplified Family Tree

others and others belong to us. We sense within us the history of our forebears and feel that we are a composite of the merging of families in our past. In coming together we have created something new by joining blood, chromosomes, genes, traditions, and histories to widen the branches of our family trees. It is a bit awesome. See the facing page for a diagram.

## Keith's Kin: His Story

The Hunts and the Wilcoxes merged with the Holmeses and the Freemans, all of whom were part of a contingent of early settlers who came from England, perhaps before the American Revolution. No one has ever bothered to find out. They settled in the midwest, in the eastern part of Michigan and finally in the town of Fenton where Ralph Hunt and Mary Ettie Holmes met in high school, fell in love, and eventually married. She was called "Pickles" and he was "Rhiney" in their high-school yearbook. They named their three sons Kenneth, Keith, and Norman Lee. Keith later married Gladys, which is how this book came into being.

Let me tell you about my family tree. My Great-Grandmother Olive Wilcox was a devout Christian, a Methodist in the good old days when John Wesley was taken seriously and the Epworth League produced disciples. We have a picture of her at age ninety, sitting in her Shaker rocking chair, making fan quilts for each of her grandchildren out of deep-colored woolen materials left over from handmade dresses and worn out trousers, carefully feather-stitching with embroidery floss along the edges of each piece. (Our daughter-in-law, a quilter and quilt-lover herself has the one we inherited hanging in the upstairs hall of her Victorian farmhouse.)

Most of what I know about this stalwart woman is from

family legend or from her diary. An entry in Olive Wilcox's diary for May 6, 1910, reads, "Today I finished setting Glenn's quilt together, and now have Ethel's blocks laid down ready to sew together; found I had to piece six more blocks. Am sorry patience is needed even in this. Lord, teach and perfect patience in all the work I do."

She was seventy-two years old. Her husband, Harrison, was seventy-three. Her entry for December 8 reads, "Fifty one years ago today I received my first letter from W*m. Henry Harrison Wilcox!*" Harrison, whom she called Pa, was in the insurance business. Olive's diary is full of Scripture, reports of church meetings, news about her sons, Herbert and Harrison, whose letters delighted her, and information about the children of her daughter, Hattie (Harriet), who lived nearby. I loved hearing her stories about Indians and always felt a special kinship to Abraham Lincoln because Great-Grandma Wilcox had gone to Toledo to see the funeral train bearing Lincoln's coffin back to Illinois.

Her daughter, Hattie, married John Hunt, referred to in the diary as Johnnie. Although Johnnie worked hard as a farmer, he never quite made it, so he later moved his family to Lansing, Michigan, where their life improved financially. Listening to the aunts, it seems Grandfather Hunt was a good man who loved Harriet, but he was a bit of a ne'er-do-well. Of course, whether Hattie ever saw him that way was another matter. The Hunts had eight children—four daughters and four sons. The daughters were remarkably strong and delightfully opinionated characters who kept the extended family together over the years.

Grandmother Hattie Hunt left the Methodist church when she suspected it was casting doubt on the Scripture, and she became a Nazarene. Grandfather Hunt was supportive but wasn't much into being a Christian, and that affected the future beliefs of their children. I don't remember much about Grandfather Hunt because he died when I was quite young.

My maternal grandparents were Henry Holmes and Alice Freeman. He was a professional calligrapher; he lettered important documents as an occupation. He died in 1912. My memories of him are confined to samples of his penmanship and a portrait of a distinguished gentleman, sporting a mustache. His death left his wife, Alice, alone with two daughters, aged eighteen and sixteen. My grandmother was not financially secure, but she was frugal. (One of her cake recipes calls for ten cents worth of nutmeats!) She worked as a mother's helper from time to time as new infants were born, and by today's standards, she lived in near-poverty but with great dignity. Yet she *bore* life, for the most part, rather than enjoying it. Each Sunday morning she walked two blocks to the Methodist church but never talked about her faith. It was a private matter.

While I was growing up my Grandmother Alice lived in a big white house on a quiet corner in Fenton, where a white, double-seated wooden swing stood along the walk under an ancient maple tree. It was fun to visit her, to fish in the millpond a block away, to sit in the swing at dusk on summer evenings, to hear the crickets and the creak of the swing and maybe the band concert down at the park. She wore her white hair in a French knot as she grew older and regularly beat three of her great-grandsons at dominoes. She said she would make quilts when she got old, not now. She died at age ninety-two, *sans quilts*, having been widowed for fifty years.

When Ralph Hunt came home from the Navy after World War I, he married his childhood sweetheart, Mary Ettie Holmes. That was his good fortune, for she was pert, fun-loving, and smart. Both Ralph and Ettie were hard workers and good planners without sacrificing their capacity to enjoy life. It was a family joke that Dad often squeezed Mom so hard that he hurt her ribs and sneezed so uninhibitedly that he scared her half to death. After they built their dream house, they lived in it one year because Dad lost his job as a chemist when the Great Depression hit. So they rented the house and returned to a flat in Detroit where Mom learned to feed four men with recipes that have since sustained the economy of our family.

When the Depression ended, the family left the city, remodeled an old farm house, planted a big garden, and raised a few chickens. My brothers and I played with Dad in the town band, and at home Mom would accompany us on the piano, playing all those wonderful John Phillip Sousa marches. The church, a big part of our life, offered more social life than spiritual nourishment; it was led by a minister bent on being erudite rather than biblical. Nevertheless, Dad regularly taught a Sunday-school class and Mom sponsored the youth group.

Meanwhile, we grew up. My older brother Ken and I served in World War II and afterward returned home to pursue our separate fortunes. Then one night life changed drastically for the Hunt family. On their way home from work, Dad (age fifty-six) and Ken were killed in a car-train accident, leaving Ken's wife with two small children and expecting a third. Mom, devastated with grief, sought her consolation in the Lord. She bought a house in town, took in her daughter-in-law and her children, and worked as a social worker for approximately ten years until retirement. She drew friends to her like bees to honey because of her positive, affirming view of life. At sixty-eight her life was cut short in a car accident. We weren't ready to lose her that soon! Shortly after that, Lee, the youngest son, and his family moved to the far West so that family closeness is now limited to a few phone calls each year and the rare visits. Mother is no longer here to tie us together.

## Gladys's Kin: Her Story

The story of my family involves the merger of four families, all of whom were Dutch immigrants only two and three generations ago—the Luurtsemas, the Schriemers, the De-Weerds, the Van Engelens. They came to seek their fortunes in the new world, these hard-working, strong-charactered people with an unshakable belief in the sovereignty of God. And they all settled in the flat, rich farm lands of western Michigan where there is almost as much sky and nearly as much water as in the Old Country.

It was in that tightly structured Christian community that Bill Schriemer met Clara DeWeerd at church one day and began those long (twenty-five mile) train rides out to her farm home in the country to court her. He soon bought a Ford Coupe that tore along at fifteen miles per hour. Eventually Bill and Clara married and named the third of their four children Gladys.

This is how it came to pass. In 1893 my paternal Great-Grandfather Tonnis Luurtsema, age fifty-one, a farmworker, left the Netherlands with five children and six pieces of luggage on the S.S. Obdam sailing out of Rotterdam. Eventually, he settled on a rented farm in the wetlands of western Michigan (after digging ditches in the city for ten cents an hour!). Seven years later, when he died of stomach cancer, his worldly possessions totaled $500. Capable Great-Grandmother Anna took charge of the family, married off her children, bought property, and lived to be seventy-one. Her offspring grew into a great clan as each of her five children bore anywhere from six to thirteen children.

Great-Grandfather Wieberen Schriemer and his wife, Jeltje, and their family of five left Friesland in the north of the Netherlands in 1889. In Grand Rapids, Michigan, they were welcomed by the Dutch of the Christian Reformed Church who had preceded them. The oldest of their five children was James, born on July 4, 1869. (Many years later my grandfather would tell us that one of the reasons he loved America was that the whole country celebrated his birthday.)

James, at twenty, was a carpenter with a budding construction business. He succeeded beyond his wildest dreams, but to his dying day he feared he might end up in the poor house (which is how he encouraged household frugality). He built a reputation as sturdy as the buildings he constructed, which were built to last through the millennium. In marrying Martha Luurtsema in 1896 (with $5 between them), he teamed up with a hard-working, loving woman who would eventually bear ten children to sit around the table where James would give thanks and read Scripture after every meal. (He joked about them being "olive plants around his table" from Psalm 128, the Dutch word sounding in English like "elephants around your table.") The oldest of their ten children was named Wieberen, after his grandfather; Americanized to Wilbur, it affectionately became Bill—my dad.

As six girls and three more boys came along, they moved to bigger houses, each one as clean as the one before. We always suspected that Grandmother Martha wiped up after us as we went out the door. She kept her basement as clean as her living room. She was always glad to see us and was one of those strong matriarchal figures that drew the clan together at every possible occasion and always on Christmas afternoon.

The other side of the Dutch connection—my maternal great-grandparents Alt and Jeanette Van Engelen and Peter and Klara DeWeerd—had come to America one generation earlier so that their children were American-born. The Van Engelens married late, had two children—Henry and Gertrude—and had the advantage of greater resources. Both great-grandparents on the Van Engelen side died before any grandchildren were born.

Great-grandparents Peter and Klara DeWeerd owned a farm on the highlands near the Van Engelens. Peter and Klara had six boys and one girl, and having a son to spare, they sent Nicholas to work for the Van Engelens. So it came to pass that Nicholas DeWeerd and Gertrude Van Engelen met, married, moved to an already paid-for farm, and named the second of their five children Clara Jeanette, after her two grandmothers.

My Grandfather Nicholas was a successful farmer who also kept a tenant house for farm help—usually occupied by a newly arrived family of Dutch immigrants. He was a stockholder in the bank, in the mill, and in the creamery from which the now famous Hudsonville ice cream originated, and he owned the first touring car in the village. He died of stomach cancer when I was four years old. The farm was let out on shares, and Grandmother Gertrude came to live next door to us until she died at age eighty-four. But that is getting ahead of the story.

When Bill Schriemer and Clara DeWeerd married in 1921, they made a choice that more than satisfied them for the rest of their lives. They began life together in a small town where Bill was a banker. Life centered around first a darling little girl that Bill called Peanuts (Ethel) and then a fat, happy boy that Bill called Tubby (Donald). A girl with red curls (Gladys) arrived just before the Depression, and another boy (Robert) came right after the Depression. Dad called it a rich man's family.

We had already moved to the edge of the city (Grand Rapids) where our large and loving clan of relatives lived. We had woods, a creek to swim in, and our own sandlot for ball games—and Dad had a bigger bank. Probably life changed most for my parents on that fateful day in history when the *banks closed,* a day I was too young to remember. Though I suppose I could be called a child of the Depression, I have only a sense of well-being about my childhood.

As we grew, life revolved around home, the school, and the church. Dad and Mom went to every football or basketball game in which their sons played or every performance in which the children had a part, cheering us on for every honor. (Usually Grandma and Grandpa Schriemer were there too for the honor part.)

At church—the Holland Baptist Church—we children listened to one Dutch sermon a month, understanding not a word while consuming and trading pink, green, and brown peppermints with each other. We did listen with understanding to the three other sermons a month. In church we were surrounded by grandparents, aunts, uncles, cousins, and everyone else was married to one of the above. Whether you said your piece well or poorly at the Christmas program, you had all the loving support any kid could ever wish for.

Eventually all four Schriemer children married. They loved the God of their ancestors. Fourteen grandchildren became the joy and rejoicing of their grandparents' hearts. Dad died at the age of seventy-four, full of good years, known and loved by each of his progeny, and Mom, at eighty-nine, still makes stylish clothes to wear and is full of good works, compassion, and love for her brood that now numbers sixty-three and growing. Her grandchildren and great-grandchildren rise up and call her blessed.

## Our Story

With our union we merged these two family lines with vows made before God and the witness of these families. We met at Michigan State University. Keith had come back after the war to finish his engineering degree and had found Gladys (Rusty), a junior majoring in journalism. For us this was not "chance" but another example of a sovereign God superintending all the meetings and marryings we've just told about.

We merged not only genes, but also traditions, talent, temperament, ideas. Dad Schriemer always read the Bible at the dinner table. Dad Hunt often read poetry, like the following, to his family after meals:

> If of the earthly goods thou art bereft
> And from thy slender store two loaves alone to
> thee are left,
> Sell one, and with the dole
> Buy hyacinths to feed thy soul.[2]

Now we read both the Bible and poetry at the table. We've added the new dimensions each has brought to our marriage, found new delights, honed each other's gifts, talked, prayed, disagreed, sang, laughed, worked, and become more and more our own persons. Our son and his family will take this heritage and weave it into something new from the threads of the old.

There's a strange, nostalgic satisfaction in recording all of this. We've laughed, sighed, remembered far more than we recorded, and asked, "Who would want to read all that?" What a motley crew makes up a *whole* family! "Pity the family that doesn't have, and cherish, at least one flamboyant eccentric!"[3] Every family has its share of homemade legends.

We forgot, for example, to tell you about how Keith's grandmother would snort in disgust over Great Aunt Alice who would act like a queen when she was as poor as a church mouse. We omitted an uncle who simply existed, unknown even by his son. There was the divorce that almost broke grandmother's heart. There was another grandmother who always told Gladys when she had on too much lipstick. And then there was the uncle who exclaimed, "Aren't we having fun!" at every clan gathering, which made us wonder if we were. We even skipped over the small brass piggy banks both grandmothers kept for Leper Work as well as Grandmother Martha's passion for Jewish missions.

Were there black sheep, straying sheep? Yes, we had those too, but it is surprising what you see when you take the long look at your family. The Psalmist said, "I have a goodly heritage," or a "delightful inheritance" (Psalm 16:6), and most of us do. A sinful one—that is something we have in common—but a good supply of grace has also allowed us to be nurtured and helped along the way. We didn't feel "smart enough" to be parents, and probably our ancestors didn't either. Yet we parented and so did they. Being a parent makes you aware of grace.

Looking at *your* family tree may give you the same sense of destiny that looking at ours gives us. Part of what they were, we now are. They are in our blood, and more than that, they have shown us how to live and how not to live as they built on their own heritage. And for either of those we ought to have some sense of gratitude.

Ever since Freud, people have been blaming their parents. They especially blame those who bore most of the grief of parenting, the ones who seem most responsible for all the minuses—mothers. It is nonsense for the most part. Dame Rebecca West was right in describing the United States as a nation of middle-age people running around complaining about their mothers. Life comes with the good and the bad, and someday our grandchildren will add other strains to this family tree. They will look back at us. They will be as *responsible* as we were to maximize the good, say thanks for it, and minimize what was lacking. At any point each of us can break the chain of negatives and build on the positives.

That may sound simplistic if you have had a tough background in which seeing the good requires a high-powered magnifying glass. But even child abuse cannot cancel out God's grace. Long before Freud and modern psychology, God was rescuing damaged people. Seeking therapy may help, but after all the insights, the regurgitation of the past, the tears, and the compassion of an understanding counselor, the choice still goes back to the individual. What choices will you make? The hatred, anger, bitterness that eats away at the inner person has to be dumped at the foot of the cross. Otherwise you are in the power of the load you carry.

Some families *are* sick, but most of their sickness came from bad choices. We look back and thank God for the good choices made by our predecessors—their faith in God, their perseverance, their integrity. For the most part, they kept the promises they made and have *uncomplicated* our lives. On the other hand, some families have made bad choices that have complicated the lives of its members. Everyone of us is doing one or the other for those who follow us. Families are important; we are held together by more than an umbilical cord.

Our nephew's wife bicycled over for lunch the other day with her little boy, Peter (named after his Great-Great-Great-Grandfather DeWeerd). While talking about family, she said, "I don't know how my mom ever learned to be such a wonderful mother to the three kids!" Then she told me her mother Virginia's story.

Virginia's mother died when she was four, and since her father remarried a woman who didn't want Virginia or her older sister, they were sent to live with their aged grandparents. Three years later when her grandmother died, her grandfather had to send them back to their father. Virginia said those three years with her godly grandparents set the course for her life and were like a protective covering for her against the vulgar language and hard life back home. The stepmother used their home as a midwifery clinic and shunted the girls off to a tiny, dark, fear-filled room in the attic. As soon as they were old enough, she sent them out as live-in household help. Without any family encouragement, Virginia began attending church, heard and received God's love in Christ, and eventually married the minister's son. She raised three children, all of whom would say, "She's been a wonderful mother!"

We hardly know what to make of such a story. It doesn't align with our theories and books about child-rearing or fit our contemporary neuroses about parenting. But it does fit into the larger family story of genes and character. It tells about a basic endurance handed down from forefathers that is not destroyed by one weak father's lack of compassion. God's grace rescued her so the line could go on. *This is the Lord's doing, and it is marvelous in our eyes*! And on that level it is everyone's story.

You are part of a family. You didn't come from nowhere. Family life is a set of *givens* that may be full of happiness or full of trouble, and it takes courage to take these *givens* and do something with them.

## The Healthy Family in an Age of Individualism

In an age of individualism we want to shout out our certainty that "Everyone needs a family!" *You* need one because you are human. A brand of pseudosophisticates today are suspicious of family structure and bad-mouth it as if it were some kind of bondage. Yet there's something incredibly sad about a world where people don't have brothers and sisters and cousins, and where, in columnist Russell Baker's words, "no family ever comes to dinner." We need to belong to other human beings, and if we don't have natural family, we need to borrow family and make appropriate commitments.

Some people make a point of moving away from family to get rid of either the commitment or the problem. They complain about all their family isn't. The uneasy, restless feeling that allows us to break commitments so easily is proof that we have lost our moorings and our sense of destiny as families. People cannot deny their families or leave them behind. The more we try to elude our families, the more we are apt to repeat their mistakes. "The family in one guise or another remains everybody's most basic hold of reality," writes Jane Howard.[4] We unravel the threads of our family history to understand ourselves and see what is solid enough to suggest a future. Our roots have turned out to be more important than we have arrogantly thought them to be.

*Healthy families have a sense of place*

Geography is part of our roots; its familiarity gives us a sense of belonging. In his book A *Place For You*, Paul Tournier talks about geography as well as emotional places. He says that before a couple marries, each should walk through the geography and memories of the other.

When our son entered the university, we went to the

orientation for parents, which turned out to be an instructive and amazingly sensitive time. "Don't change his room," said the head of Student Counseling. "Leave everything in its place. Don't think that you can change houses now that he is on his own; don't move if you don't have to. Your son or daughter needs to come home and find his or her room. No matter how independent children may appear to be, familiar surroundings give a sense of belonging." Ten years later we still call that room in our house "Mark's room." We really took that man seriously!

Place is important because of memories, roots, feelings, history. Moving elsewhere may provide a nicer climate or better scenery, but its value as home must also be weighed.

### Home is a safe place

Someone said, "Home is a place where when you go there, they always take you in." At home you are free to be who you are; you are safe from attack. Home should be a fortress against all the stress of the world. It is a center of morale. Otherwise, it is only a house where you live.

Your home may be light-years from this description, but this definition is still a worthy goal. Safe places are made by safe people. Strong families are made up of people who are safe to be with. Such families have individuals like you and me who need to deal with our inability to accept others, our selfishness, and our lack of self-control.

A family is a unit of people who belong to each other by marriage (choice) and by birth (no choice) and who are committed to care for each other as long as they live. Not all families are composed of blood relatives. Ideally, a family needs both a father and a mother. As children grow older the love of a mother, in some wonderful way, has an affirming, settling affect on sons, and fathers give that same message of worth and personhood to daughters. In addition, each models the potential of manhood and womanhood. A boy wants to be competent like his father, and a girl desires the same as she watches her mother. Each wants to grow up like the model parent and be loved by someone like the opposite parent.

But family is more than what Martin Marty calls "two parents and two children and sometimes a psychiatrist." We need the *clan*—aunts, uncles, grandparents, cousins, nieces, and nephews. And if we don't have our own nearby in this age of mobility, we need to adopt some. We adopt all kinds of people into our family: extra children to make up for the eight we didn't have, parents who don't have children, nieces and nephews. Why not? Love is more stretchy and the heart has more room on the inside than most people think. We need the blend of ages and that intergenerational feel in families. We *must* make certain that our children know older people in the midst of our youth culture.

Gladys went to the hospital to see her father one day before his surgery. She sat on the edge of the bed as they talked together. At one point he held out his arm and said, "Honey, whose old-looking arm is this? Surely it can't be mine!" She saw in a trice that he was nineteen inside, and into her mind came the picture of her father coming home with a bouquet of wild flowers he had picked for her mother. He had a hole in his trousers where he had caught them in the barbed-wire fence he had climbed. How much information and how many fascinating stories have been missed because people know only their peers. Aunts and uncles are missed because they seem blurred roles like librarians or viceroys. Not ours! They made the chief cheering section in our growing-up days.

Thankfully, grandparents are in much more abundant

supply than they were a generation or two ago when life expectancy was shorter. Every child ought to know his grandparents. Healthy grandparents are affirming adults in children's lives. Since they take in a larger view of life, they are more forgiving of the foibles that exasperate parents. They have a lifetime of wisdom to share, time for games and stories, and are good at keeping confidences. If actual grandparents are not close, a family shouldn't find it too hard to find substitutes. One church we know makes an official ritual out of adopting grandparents, a ceremony that is especially meaningful to one-parent families. Grandparenting is so exhilarating that one of our friends suggested skipping the parenting part and getting right on with having grandchildren.

*Strong families have some founder or matriarch as their center*

The founder calls the family together, keeps people connected by information, and carries out these duties by dint of personality and commitment. No one votes such a person into office; a person just assumes the role. Every family needs someone in the center who keeps all the news clippings and family pictures. Usually this is a mother. Then it becomes a sister or the clan gatherings cease. We have observed that if it were up to the "men folk," most families would seldom meet and few would receive birthday cards, though this generalization is sometimes false.

Geography often puts an enormous barrier between people of the same family. If they don't write or call regularly, they have less and less in common. Martin Marty comments that if you write someone a letter daily you cannot end the pages, but if you write annually, there will be less to say each year. Although the telephone has made for easy communication, a disembodied voice is no substitute for face-to-face conversation. It is best to travel that extra distance, and it is nice if visits don't have to be negotiated. Barriers disappear when you feel at home enough to get a carrot stick out of the refrigerator and know where the butter is kept.

### Healthy families are affectionate

Every child needs to grow up with someone who is absolutely wild about him or her. Or as family ecologist Dr. Urie Bronfenbrenner puts it, everyone needs to grow up with someone who has an irrational commitment to his well-being.[5] Grownups need the same thing. That is what makes being a grandparent so special. The vulnerable experiences in life—loss, loneliness, the dependency of advanced age— must matter to someone. Old as well as young people need to be hugged, kissed, and touched. It is such a basic human need, and we are suddenly acting as if we had discovered a new drug after finding that studies show that everyone needs at least four hugs a day.

Someone commented to a boy who was carrying his brother on his back, "That's quite a load, isn't it?" The boy replied, "He's not heavy; he's my brother." Family affection includes this bearing one another up, this knowing that your sister will care and your brother will help.

### Healthy families accept one another

The most common battleground in families is an inability to really accept the other person. Expectations are too high; sometimes they are unreal. Other times expectations are too low; there is nothing to live up to. Accepting things and people means accepting them *the way they are* rather than pretending they are the way you want them to be.

Acceptance of others need not include approval of all they do. It is easy to give a superficial acceptance, but when behavior is disappointing and sometimes downright wrong, acceptance becomes a deep crisis event. Grace and understanding, mercy, forgiveness: These are all Christian words. They are more than words; they are the very qualities we have experienced from a perfect and righteous God. As God has been to us, says John White in his helpful book *Parents in Pain*,[6] so we must be to others in the tough affairs of family life.

Think of the husbands and wives at each other's throats, the parent-child hostility, the brother-brother rejection. "We have left undone those things which we ought to have done, and we have done those things which we ought not to have done. But thou, O Lord, have mercy on us . . . spare us, restore us for thy name's sake."

Our expressions of love are not as true as we might think sometimes. "I always did this or that, but he cheated me, . . ." or "Look at the things I've done for her, and this is the way I've been treated. . . ." Being realistic about our own sin before attempting to work on someone else's is the plain teaching of the Sermon on the Mount. Misinterpreting the instruction from Jesus about specks and planks (Matthew 7:3–5) has paralyzed people from helping either themselves or others with a kind of doubtful neutrality about all sin. And it thwarts acceptance. The teaching says, *First handle your own . . . then help your brother remove* . . . The order is important; but both are necessary.

God's gift of forgiveness brought about our own renewal and mending. We *must* pass this on in finite ways to those in our families. God uses every act of genuine love, and love is always according to truth; it has a standard. Love does not mean anyone can do as he pleases. Family life calls us to repentance, to forgiveness (not pretending), to genuine evaluation of our own behavior, and to concern for "the spirit" and not just the outward behavior.

## Becoming an Untroubled Family

Family therapist Virginia Satir classifies families as being either open or closed systems. Within each system she gives four elements that determine family life: *self-worth*, the feelings and ideas one has about oneself; *communication*, the ways people work to make meaning with one another; *rules*, the system people use for how they should feel and act; and *link to society*, the way people relate to other people and institutions outside the home. No matter what kind of problems a family has, Satir has found that help comes in changing one of these four key factors. This is how she sees nurturing families and troubled families:[7]

| Key Factor | Nurturing Family | Troubled Family |
| --- | --- | --- |
| Self-worth | high | low |
| Communication | direct, clear, honest | indirect, vague, dishonest |
| Rules | flexible, human, appropriate, subject to change | rigid, inhuman, non-negotiable, everlasting |
| Link to Society | open and hopeful | fearful, placating, blaming |

These insights seem so obvious as to provoke wonder that every troubled family doesn't jump from the troubled column into the nurturing one. Certainly, a proper view of being made in the image of God and the good sense of human consistency *presumes* all the elements of a nurturing family. But, alas, we are a fallen people. The confusion brought about by sin has complicated family life. Yet at any point, the grace of God and one's own commitment can break negative patterns and enforce the positive links of the happy family.

*The esteem factor*

Low self-esteem leads to poor communication, which leads to rigidity of rules for family operation. Some people have been taught by well-meaning ministers or parents that God views all of us as worthless and so full of sin that the only appropriate "Christian" attitude is self-reproach: "Such a worm as I. . . ." Taking inventory of their own hearts, some don't find this teaching hard to believe, especially if the heart is full of resentment and insecurity from being put down as hopeless since birth. On the other end of the spectrum, our absorption with self in today's culture is as full of error as the demeaning of one's self. Since our enemy loves to get us off the main road, either ditch will do! Nowhere in Holy Scripture is the idea of worthlessness taught. Instead the message of the Bible is encapsulated in the story of the Shepherd who rescues the lost sheep at great cost to himself. His glad song is, "Rejoice, for I have found my sheep!"

The pattern for low self-esteem is sometimes cut out of theological cloth that says people are as bad as they can be. "Make sure they stay in line. At the sign of any softness or grace, they will take advantage of you." In families where this belief translates into rigid rules—"I'll love you *if* . . ."— there is fear that praise or affirmation will spoil the child. Give this pattern a few generations to break people apart, and some very sad distortions of family life emerge.

Out of this witch's brew of fear and authoritarianism has come child abuse, wife abuse, and the victimizing of one's own family members. Studies show that sexual abuse and incest within families most often comes from authoritarian males who tend to be very moralistic and conservative in their religious beliefs. They also believe they "own" their women. They are often regular church attenders. Family or marital stress, poor communication, lack of warmth and acceptance within the home are the seed beds for tragic behavior. This is particularly true if a person has limited control of his or her impulses or is subject to obsessional thinking. When researchers claim that as many as twenty-five percent of college-age women had sexual activity with family members during childhood and adolescence, we can justifiably be appalled at the depth to which family life can sink.

The profile of the abusive father reads like this: "He is intelligent, a good provider, religious, but he has a poor self-concept and lacks full control of his impulses; he is socially isolated, feels needy and neglected, lacks intimacy in his life; his marriage is not satisfying; and he was abused or emotionally neglected as a child. In other words, he is not a 'crazed sex pervert.' "[8] He is the needy guy who may live next door or in your house.

Who better than family can provide feelings of self-worth? Where can you better learn how to communicate and find out how to live with human beings? The family needs to be reinforced with open, honest dialogue about feelings and intimacy and rules and sexuality. We cannot control the behavior of another, but we can contribute to it.

*Child raising*

The Bible contains instruction for all people, giving them principles by which to live. Fathers are told, "Do not exasperate your children; instead, bring them up in the *training* and *instruction* of the Lord" (Ephesians 6:4, italics ours). Parents are told not to withhold discipline (Proverbs 23:13–14), which is not an excuse for child-beating but an encouragement to help a child toward inner self-control. "Character is a plant that grows more sturdily for some cutting back."[9] The book of Proverbs, says Kidner, is well-known for its praise of the rod, but less well-known for its own reasonable approach, affectionate witness, and assumption that the old find their natural crown and the young their proper pride in each other.

"Train a child in the way he should go, and when he is old he will not turn from it" (Proverbs 22:6). This is not a promise that the child will become a Christian. The training prescribed is literally "according to the child's way," implying, it seems, respect for his individuality and vocation, though not for his self-will.[10] The implications of that teaching necessitate sensitivity to the child's person. A sensitive child, for example, may need help in distinguishing between acceptance and approval. They are not the same thing and parents must make clear that acceptance is *steadfast*; approval depends on behavior. And both involve love. Right and wrong are important teachings. The kind of discipline advocated takes the "child's way" seriously. Some children are broken-hearted by a stern look; another child needs a spanking to get the message.

The most beautiful picture of parental training is given in Deuteronomy 6:6–8 where fathers and mothers teach their children the truth about God and his rules for living all day long—in their walks together and their talks together, at breakfast and at bedtime. It is as if truth were written on the doorposts of the house they live in. That means parent-child times together take precedence over television and other activities. Psalm 78 gives the goal: that they may set their hope in God and tell *their* children and *their* grandchildren the works of God, so that each generation will have a steadfast, faithful heart toward God. "It is, after all, God's name that generations exist to proclaim, not their own. Our own names, our own stories must be entrusted to a more able recorder than ourselves or our children...." Nevertheless, we are allowed to make a mark on the lives of others by obeying

God. Family is one of the ways God maintains a witness to himself in this world.[11]

Surely the gifts parents want to give their children include self-esteem, trust, consistency, understanding and compassion, limits for moral and spiritual safety, and corrective discipline. Rigid parents give their children too many unnecessary things to rebel against. Permissive parents give no training in respect, in the curbing of impulsive behavior, or in the safety of boundaries. Children cannot learn grace until they learn law, says Joe Bayly. We must teach our children righteousness and justice as we show mercy appropriately. A child's conscience is trained by discipline; he should be able to be self-controlled by the age of twelve.

Nowhere does the Bible explain how to produce the perfect family in seven easy steps. It tells us we are made in the image of God, gives principles for working out that responsibility in a fallen world, and demonstrates the parenting of God.

It is far easier for parents to try to be godly (godlike) than to try to produce perfect children. Being godly is a responsibility you can handle with God's grace. Your child's response is his responsibility. The parenting of God teaches us that.

Father is the divine name only *lent* to creatures. God the Father thought up families for us to teach us something of who *he* is. Because we have been parents ourselves, we can understand how God is vulnerable to the cries of his children, even in their sins. "Is there any other way we could have understood a God who suffers except by means of this eternal Father and Son who make of every mortal relationship a metaphor?"[12]

*Parent honoring*

Children have their own set of responsibilities. The foremost of these is to honor their father and mother. This is so important that the biblical instruction comes with a promise "so that you may live long. . . ." It is the only one of the ten commandments without "thou shalt not." It is positive action and a matter of the heart. It doesn't exempt anyone from honor if their parents are beastly or neurotic or troublemakers. Honor is different from obedience. Children are to obey their parents (Ephesians 6:1). Honor is not something we grow out of, but something we grow into. One appreciates its import as you grow older and see its implications.

The woman down the street who does all kinds of volunteer work at the hospital but can't find time to go see her parents—she may be you, forgetting about honoring. Sons too busy even to phone; that may be you. After retirement, when the postman brings fewer and fewer pieces of mail, have you seen Dad at the mailbox waving a letter and calling out to Mother, "It's from James!" Honoring may mean writing a letter, caring enough to spend an afternoon, listening to a story you've heard before. Whatever the form, honoring is a "holding in great respect."

John Howe tells a parable about an old man who lived with his married son and daughter-in-law. His hands trembled; he had trouble eating; and he usually spilled things. So they made him a little table out in back. One day the couple noticed their own son playing with bits of wood. They asked what he was doing, and he said, "I'm making a little table where I can feed you when I get big."[13] Honor your father and your mother. It is a big principle. The instruction assumes you will find creative expressions of this from out of your own heart.

Human families don't always provide every one with the glowing feeling of belonging. The best of families can only do so much. Someone said good families are much to all their members, but everything to none. Troubled families may seem to provide more tears and pain than anything else. But in God's tender care for us we are not limited to earthly families. God gives everyone a "goodly heritage" in the best sense of that phrase. It is called the family of God, and he is the Father, of whom all other fathers are only pale reflections. This family has brothers and sisters who are joined together in Christ, "members of one another," as Scripture says. This family often provides closer ties than blood relatives. Within the church we find the grandparents we never knew, the mothering and fathering we've missed, and the wide spectrum of extended family we've always wanted. Some of them will be as eccentric, as complex, and as annoying as any born in our natural families. But that only emphasizes the diversity in God's grace.

Best of all is the sense of belonging to an eternal Parent, our Father in heaven, God Almighty, Maker of heaven and earth. We look at our shriveled lives, hope for a miracle of love and healing, and hear the angel's words: "Is anything too hard for the LORD?" (Genesis 18:14). Then if we come close and let him love us, he tells us that he has chosen us to be his own inheritance before we were even in our mother's womb. And our inner spirit cries out, "Abba, Father."

---

[1] Robert Nathan, *So Love Returns* (New York: Alfred A. Knopf, Inc., 1958), 138.

[2] Sadi (*Nom de plume* of Sharh-a-DIN), *The Home Book of Quotations*, Burton Stevenson, ed. (New York: Dodd, Mead and Co., 1964), 945.

[3] Jane Howard, *Families* (New York: Simon and Schuster, 1978), 31.

[4] Ibid., 242.

[5] Urie Bronfenbrenner, "The American Family," from a tape in The Harvard Seminar Series (Cambridge: Harvard University Press, 1981).

[6] John White, *Parents in Pain* (Downers Grove, Ill.: InterVarsity Press, 1979), 209.

[7] Virginia Satir, *Peoplemaking* (Palo Alto, Calif.: Science and Behavior Books, Inc., 1972), 3.

[8] Richard E. Butman, "Hidden Victims," HIS magazine, April 1983, 21.

[9] Derek Kidner, *Proverbs* (London: Tyndale, 1964), 51.

[10] Ibid., 147.

[11] Virginia Stem Owens, A *Feast of Families* (Grand Rapids: Zondervan Publishing House, 1983), 42.

[12] Ibid., 130, 131.

[13] John W. Howe, "The Real Story Behind the Fifth," from *Your Family* (Downers Grove, Ill.: InterVarsity Press, 1982), 19.

*chapter* 7

# Committed

Marriage is a subject of such enormous importance that we approach it with awe. So much can be said about it; indeed, so much has already been written about it. Of all relationships, this one as "bane or blessing" involves the most lasting consequences, affects the largest number of people, and is the most crucial to the establishment of an orderly, productive society.

Marriage is more than sexual urges driving two people to make a commitment to each other. It involves dreams, the building of people, the establishment of *home* (one of the most emotionally effective words in our language), and the provision of total care for the total person.

But it is even more than this. Marriage is ordained by God. He made the first bride and gave her to the first man, thus making a powerful statement about human design and need. Long before "parenting" was made into a biblical concept, the Scripture records that a man leaves his father and mother and is united to his wife and they become one flesh. God also introduces the concept of *unity*, which comes out of his own nature: two become one.

And it is a unity based on equality. Despite the almost universal acceptance of the translation of Genesis 2:18b of the woman as a "helper suitable" for man, Dr. R. David Freedman, in his extensive study of the Hebrew words *ezer knegdo* (which describe the to-be-created woman), states that these words should be translated to mean approximately "a power equal to man." That is, when God created another creature so that man would not be alone, he made someone whose strength—not merely physical power—was equal to the man's. Woman was not intended to be man's helper. She was to be instead his partner.[1]

The woman has the same essential being as the man, although she brings to the relationship a complementary nature so that she is both equal and different. Created in the image of God, husband and wife together reflect the community that exists within the Godhead. An interdependence exists between them that neither can escape; it is God's doing.

But marriage is even more. In some mysterious way the uniting of two people in marriage and their pledge of fidelity to each other is a reflection of divine love. Marriage mirrors the relationship of Christ and the church. It is an earthly picture of the spiritual relationship between God and mankind. So many relational facets are found in the symbol: the headship of the husband; the submission of the wife; the loving nurture and sacrificial self-giving of the husband; the loving respect and fidelity of the wife. This picture of covenant-keeping is a sacred mystery with profound implications for the way *we* treat each other and live together (see Ephesians 5:32). In essence, each person in the couple says to the other, "As God has been to me, so I must be to you. As Christ and the church belong to each other, so we belong to each other."

This "great mystery" needs to be carefully considered. God's covenant keeping and fidelity to his people is the model for the marriage relationship. Godly people reflect God's way of keeping promises. God made a commitment to be "Husband" to his people and to accept them as his own through thick and thin. He took his people for richer for poorer, for better for worse, in sickness or in health. "I will betroth you to me forever" (Hosea 2:19). The long story of God's marriage to Israel in the Old Testament is the story of God's faithfulness to his vow, a faithfulness often tested by Israel's wanderings. His was no legalistic bargain or commitment only to a contract. He had the welfare of his beloved in mind; he sought Israel's good. And who knew what that good was better than he, the Creator? God's faithfulness meant *relationship* with his people; he wanted them to find their identity in him. The Lord God became the Lover, the Bridegroom, the Husband.

Moreover, as Lewis Smedes has pointed out, when God "got married" to one nation, he wanted to bless all the nations of the earth. The fidelity within his relationship to Israel was meant to provide a redemptive ministry to those outside the partnership. In a similar way, a healthy marriage emanates refreshment and nourishment to those whose lives touch their partnership. The open hand and open heart that shares life's goodness and the Good News with others is the kind of hospitality God approves.

The story of the New Testament is the completion of this faithful love of God. The lover becomes the sacrifice, the Savior, and the Redeemer. In final triumph he calls to himself the bride, the church of Christ—some from every tribe and nation—that all history might be summed up in this steadfast love of God. The story brings to completion the plan made before the foundation of the world, the plan of an indissoluble union of Christ and the church consummated at a marriage supper in heaven:

> Let us rejoice and be glad and give him glory!
> For the wedding of the Lamb has come,
> and his bride has made herself ready.
>
> (Revelation 19:7)

The now-revealed mystery is the relationship of Christ and the church. "The intimate husband-wife partnership throws light upon the covenant between Christ and His bride. Similarly, the faithfulness of God, the divine Husband, or Christ, the faithful Bridegroom, throws light on what marriage can and should be."[2] It is the full partnership and communion of lover and beloved. Whenever love and marriage reflect the will of God in this way, the aim of creation is proclaimed and this reflection mirrors God's faithfulness to his children throughout the history of mankind. Marriage involves destiny, the will of God, the fulfilling of his purposes. We say something about God in the way we live together. What an enormous concept! What cosmic importance! And some of us thought marriage was just a stirring of impulses, an erotic attraction, the thing to be done, a choosing of our own.

## Keeping Vows

Who knows all the significance the years will give the vows made before God and a company of witnesses on the wedding day? A vow is a positive statement of trust in the face of all the uncertainties the future holds. This trust involves loyalty, devotion, reliability, and love. *Troth* is the Old English word that captures the positive aspects of marriage vows. Troth means truth. "I pledge you my truth." At its core is integrity, trust, fidelity, and authenticity.

The call to troth making, according to James Olthuis, is a unique dimension of the call to be human.[3] A life of troth, in our minds, is a life that evidences that we are made in the image of God. When people live in troth they can count on each other; it leads to intimacy and understanding. Troth is the moral expression of love; it is possible because we are made moral beings who are capable of commitment and choice.

When we marry we make the vows of troth or fidelity. It is the intentional side of a relationship. We vow that "for better or worse" we will not let circumstances or feelings dictate the future of our marriage. Lewis Smedes reminds us that "loyalty to a vow cannot turn a commitment to endurance into a happy marriage, but *intentional faithfulness to a promise* once made can sustain the possibility for a re-creation of the marriage. Vows stand as a reminder that marriage is based on more than eros."[4]

Fidelity is more than a commitment not to break the seventh commandment ("thou shalt not commit adultery"); it is a commitment to one's partner as a human being. It is a calling to dedicate self to the task of creating an environment in which the other can become all God means that person to be.

This needs to be said loudly and clearly in this day of transient marriages and loveless relationships. More than the mere absence of adultery or gritting one's teeth in cold endurance is required in the marriage troth. Instead, marriage is a partnership God himself created, "so that the continuation of the marriage is not up to human choice and desire alone. Two people chose each other as partners; but God willed the partnership they enter."[5] The call of God is to make the relationship into a real marriage and to work through the hard places toward new understanding and transparency. Such a *becoming* together includes a smoothing of rough edges and a changing of impossible habits with the help of the one who superintended the vows. The institution of marriage, rightly understood, sustains the opportunity for this kind of creative partnership. Our capacity for faithfulness makes the marriage vow possible; our propensity to selfishness makes it necessary.

Not all stories of faithfulness are as dramatic as this one, but it serves to illustrate the safety and the humanness of keeping vows. A young wife, five years into marriage and the mother of two small children, developed multiple sclerosis. When her condition worsened and she was confined to a wheelchair, her husband continued his work and began doing the household chores—cooking, cleaning, laundry.

Then her medication caused her to bloat; she felt ugly and unattractive in every way. She suspected that even her personality had changed. After several years of this she became so discouraged she made a decision. When her husband came home that evening she laid her conclusions before him: "John, you didn't plan a life like this when you married me. You are young. Take the children and leave me. Find a good woman who will be to you the wife I wanted to be."

John was silent for a time and then asked, "If I had MS would you leave me?" Of course she would not, she replied. "That's your answer," said John. And they never talked about it again. John had learned and taught something about vow keeping.[6]

Dietrich Bonhoeffer said, "Our love makes the marriage and then our marriage keeps the love." The vows we make hold us steady in troubled times. Another of our friends felt like a noose around her husband's neck when she developed polio during an epidemic in Australia. She shared this feeling with her husband who wisely pointed out, "This has not just happened to *you*. This has happened to *us*." He was affirming biblical oneness.

But, you may say, these are the heroic moments when courage rises to the fore. What of the little annoyances, the dissatisfactions that deplete a relationship bit by bit? It is true about "little foxes that ruin the vineyards" (Song of Songs 2:15). But that is why we need the holy triangle we will discuss next.

## A Practical Look at Marriage

The strangest teachings about marriage have been stuffed into Bible passages and given a Christian veneer. They are system-oriented, with seven how-to steps that can be taught in seminars; they are role conscious. One theory is essentially male domination of women whose only link to God is through a man. Another espouses a sex-bomb approach in the name of Christian marriage; the underlying idea is that wives can count on their husband's infidelity unless they "put out."

These are not troth marriages. Instead they are an absorption with personal insecurity and fear that Christian marriage is no different from secular marriage. Another system would have us dethrone men so that women could be enthroned. And there are other systems that try with their formulas to treat the troubled relationships so evident all around us.

Christian marriage worthy of the name is on a different level entirely. First of all, it consciously has a third partner; it is the only triangle within marriage that works.

The obvious teaching of the triangle is that the closer the man and the woman are to God, the closer they are to each other. Walter Trobisch defined a similar diagram as a tent in which the husband and wife dwell safely.[7] Christian marriage assumes love and loyalty to God; he cannot be ignored if the relationship is to function. Why ignore the designer of marriage? Marriage is too big for two people. If we have any concept of our constant need of forgiveness and reconciliation as fallen creatures, we will daily affirm the importance of God's presence in our marriage. The Scripture says, "A cord of three strands is not quickly broken" (Ecclesiastes 4:12).

Second, Christian marriage is person-centered, not system-centered. For each partner it is other-centered; yet it is not a denial of self. Each is free to be who he is, freer than ever before because of the safety of marriage troth. Yet each is concerned for the other. Anne Morrow Lindbergh defines it this way in her book *Gift from the Sea*: "A good relationship has a pattern like a dance and is built on some of the same rules. The partners do not need to hold on tightly, because they move confidently in the same pattern, intricate but gay and swift and free, like a country dance of Mozart's. There is no place here for the possessive clutch, the clinging arm, the heavy hand; only the barest touch in passing. Now arm in arm, now face to face, now back to back—it does not matter. Because they know they are partners moving to the same rhythm, creating a pattern together, and being invisibly nourished by it."[8]

It is a strange mixture of dependence, independence, and interdependence. There is independence within unity. Each person is becoming more who they were really meant to be (independence) in the climate of love and acceptance of the other (dependency). And in the process of growth, there is a refinement in communication of who they are (their ideas, dreams, concerns, vulnerabilities) so that they experience the oneness (interdependency) the Scriptures talk about.

**Person          Spouse**

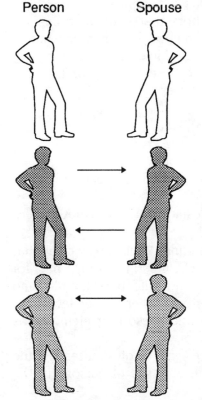

*Independence*: You must grow as individuals.

*Dependence*: Your spouse provides the climate for that growth by loving you, and vice versa.

*Interdependence*: You share what is happening inside you, and the experience of *oneness* grows with the refinement of your communication.

Each gives; each receives. This is no fifty-fifty bargaining arrangement. A beautiful mutuality is the hallmark of Christian marriage. Each offers the other the freedom to be who they are; each helps the maturing of the other and in the process experiences more personal maturity; each provides a climate for growth.

In his Ephesian letter, the Apostle Paul raised so high a standard for human behavior that it ought to startle us each time we read what it means to relate as a member of God's family. It is no small thing to be told to imitate God as a child does a father (Ephesians 5:1–2), especially when that Father has given himself up as a sacrifice in Christ. The careful lifestyles of such imitators that Paul describes cut across the grain of life in the Roman world even more sharply than it does in our own culture. God lives in you by the Holy Spirit, Paul instructs; now let the Spirit fill your life, and when he does you will find yourselves

> speaking together about the Lord
> singing to our Lord
> thanking God through our Lord
> submitting to one another out of reverence for our
>   Lord.
>                    (Ephesians 5:19–21 paraphrased)

In the event of misunderstanding, Paul makes clear that this lifestyle is not for church meetings only, but for relationships in the home (husband, wife, parent, child) and in the marketplace (slaves, masters). Whenever believers are together one would expect to find these four elements as evidence of the life of God in them.

The examples he proceeded to give revolutionized Gentile life with its emphasis on the importance of persons in the sight of God. Imitating God by a self-sacrificing life is not an exercise in martyrdom, but children following the Father's example in concern for others.

The example of marriage has particular relevance. Wives are given three verses of instructions (5:22–24), and husbands are given six verses (5:25–30). The instructions are carefully addressed to each party. (Husbands are not told to make their wives submit, and wives are not to make their husbands love, for example.) Both instructions involve the self-sacrifice that should characterize the Father's children, which Paul calls submission.

Wives are told to make their lives subject to the needs of their husbands, and to do so with respect for Christ in mind. "Inasmuch as you have done this . . . you have done it to me." In his Colossian letter, Paul uses the phrase "as is fitting in the Lord" (3:18). Live up to the Christian standard, he is saying, the standard for the role to which Christ has called you.

Husbands are instructed to love as Christ loved the church, with *agape*, the self-giving love. The husband is given the high calling of following Christ's example in his goals that the church might be

> sanctified
> cleansed
> all potential realized
> beautiful.

That is how men ought to love their wives and meet their needs so they can become all they were meant to be. If that seems too lofty, Paul helps us by reminding us that the church is the body of Christ. No one hates his own body, but nourishes it and cherishes it. Love your wives, says Paul, as you love yourself.

Nowhere in this Ephesian passage, so often read at weddings, is the word "authority" used. The examples are all in the model of the self-giving love of Christ, for both husbands and wives.

Yet the text does say, "For the husband is the head of the wife as Christ is the head of the church." What does it mean to be "head"? People in our culture immediately think of "head of a company," the corporate model—the one who runs the outfit and makes the decisions. But recently some scholars, spurred on by the feminist movement, have studied "head" as it is used in the Scripture and have concluded that *head* means *source* or *fountainhead*. As Christ is the source of the Church, the fountainhead from which it sprang, so woman was made from man who is thus her source. Whatever the conclusion, certainly the example used does not so much point to authority in decision-making as self-giving and *responsibility* for the other person. There is both authority and sacrifice in taking responsibility, but it is not authoritarianism or domination.

James Olthuis calls headship a special office of service so that the marriage may thrive and grow.[9] Husbands and wives must be committed to moving in the same direction with a common life vision, he says, because a marriage divided against itself cannot stand. They must call each other to live up to their dreams, and in particular, the husband must assume responsibility to take inventory on the growth and refinement of their relationship to keep the marriage on track. That kind of headship would receive wifely applause without question.

The husband as "head" is a biblical idea; so is submission. Those words raise the hackles of many today and are grossly overstated by others of a more traditional stance. Isn't that simply a commentary on our refusal to serve someone else?

When Paul wrote those words they were liberating and uplifting and spoke of quality relationships that reflect the kind of lifestyle that the Father had taught his children. We think they do the same for contemporary society when rightly understood.

## The Satisfaction of Relating

Christian marriage is troth: a vow made before God. It is God-centered, person-centered, and other-centered. It is also a satisfying relationship. That is why so many people who know little about God long to be married and stay married even when elements of pain confound its pleasure. There is the satisfaction and sheer fun of growing together, of having someone to surprise, of understanding private jokes, of the sexual relationship, of someone who reaches for your hand when you roll over in bed at night. Then there is the excitement of a new baby who is a part of each of you, the product of your love—your own private miracle.

God means marriage to be pleasure and joy. God is the author of all pleasure. This is never more evident than when we contemplate our sexual design, such as the way a man and his wife fit together physically or the sensitive nerve endings in the parts of our bodies that are designed for marriage pleasure. We forget sometimes that sex is a gift from God, not something man discovered and can exploit in any way he pleases—even within marriage. The devil, incapable of creating anything, can only distort what already exists. He has found all areas of pleasure to be a fertile field for his talents.

In Christian marriage we make a commitment to live with reality, not fantasy. Today's easy access to pornography of all kinds necessitates a clear statement about the danger of being hooked on unreality. Newspaper columnists may encourage fantasizing about another person to make sexual intercourse more meaningful within marriage, but you will be hurt if you believe that. Fantasy is no substitute for reality. Instead it is a kind of infidelity that will keep a marriage from the intimacy it deserves. Sex means seeking the genuine relationship, not sensations. The centerfold of a porn magazine can keep you from experiencing the satisfaction of reality.

*Thinking right* ("whatever is right, whatever is pure . . . think about such things," Philippians 4:8) is essential for a full life, and we must deal with anything in our secret lives that keeps us from that. God never meant for sex to be that dark, hidden, guilt-ridden area in life. He encourages us not to be "closet" anything. He who sees in secret and knows the heart can also deliver from the confusion of a demon-ridden view of sexuality. We will *not* die without sex, despite the propaganda of the media. We *will* wither and die without genuine relationships.

The sexual relationship within marriage, when rightly understood, has a holy aura about it. It is a deep way of giving to each other, a way of expressing physical oneness that already exists in the emotional and practical areas of life. Without the interweaving of two personalities and the self-giving we have discussed, the sex act is only that: a sexual act. Its potential for expression is limited to the act itself. Sex, buttressed by the sense of well-being that mutual emotional support provides, becomes deep communication and a profound way of belonging to each other.

The seemingly endless discussion about sex in our culture and the plethora of books on sexual technique have not resulted in happier or more fulfilled marriages. Elaborate prescriptions for orgasms and positions and whatever have only resulted in less concern for the persons and more concern for sensations. Indeed the sexual experience when so deified inevitably proves to be disillusioning and unsatisfying in the long run. Pleasure for pleasure's sake is a distortion of its purpose; all true pleasure is an expression of a higher truth.

Relationship is again the key. "Sex can be free only within a relationship rooted in something beyond sex."[10] Any human action involves the total person whether we consciously acknowledge this or not. What is needed is not more sex education but more troth education. Olthuis says that troth intercourse needs to be blended with physical intercourse if the sexual part of marriage is to be meaningful.[11] He is pleading for the kind of totality of involvement, vulnerability, and intimacy that makes two people one.

We are not advocating a return to a Victorian silence about sex and sexuality. Rather we would encourage a fresh look at what it means to be human and what really satisfies in life. Rollo May comments that modern man has taken the fig leaf off the genitals and has put it over the face. We protest the depersonalization of sex that makes it sensuous rather than relational. At its best, sex is both. But even at its best it cannot bear the whole weight of a relationship. It is not insignificant that human beings are the only creatures who can mate face to face and talk about their love expressions both during intercourse and afterward. We are made to *relate* to each other and to meet each other's needs in this both serious and playful aspect of married life.

And there must be a playful side to our relationships within marriage, lest we take ourselves too seriously or become solemnly ritualistic instead of romantic and frivolous in love. Happy are those couples who can laugh at themselves, accept each other, and talk about every part of their life together, including sex. It is they who can make their marriage union a "safe place" because of their commitment to each other.

With the advent of effective contraception, conceiving children has become a secondary issue in sexual relationship. Yet conception is an important part of marriage satisfaction and is intimately related to the sexual life of a married couple. The need to contrive ways to keep from conceiving indicates how profoundly sex is related to childbearing. To make a decision to have no children, as some are doing today, is to go against the likely fruit of sexual union and raises some haunting questions for the couple who make such a choice. Are self-doubts or self-absorption bringing on such a decision (excluding medical reasons, of course)? Will such a choice affect the endurance and depth of a partnership? Are fears keeping you from such a commitment? Is this using freedom responsibly?

A couple must ask hard questions if they are to be morally responsible in this area. The world is in sad shape, but that is reason enough to raise godly children. Pessimism is not compatible with faith. Our children are the people God will use in what he purposes to do in the world. Sorrow and hurts *may* come with the raising of children. It is one of the risks of love.

Yet the bearing of children is not the reason for either marriage or sexual pleasure. The most significant verse about marriage in the Bible, quoted four times, tells us that "a man will leave his father and mother and be united to his wife, and they will become one flesh" (Genesis 2:24). Nothing is said about children. Marriage is significant not because it produces children but because of the "one flesh" union that mirrors the community within the Godhead and God's relationship with his church. Hurts that come from childlessness are difficult enough. We need a clear understanding that neither sex nor children can bear the weight of a marriage. A good marriage necessitates the kind of communication that makes two people one. Genuine love is what marriage is all about.

### Hard Places in Marriage

*Communication.* Communication remains the biggest single factor in determining a happy marriage relationship. When a couple have developed good communication skills, the most serious of their problems fade. The difficulty is that communication skills in two people rarely match.

In a newspaper column entitled "The Rejection of Intimacy,"[12] Ellen Goodman tells of a couple seated near her in a restaurant eating dinner. The wife was looking at the man; he was looking at his plate. Engaging him with a half-smile, cocking her head flirtatiously, the wife finally asked her husband what he was thinking about. He returned her smile and said, "Oh, nothing," and went back to his dinner. With a hint of hurt, his wife pierced a heart of lettuce and joined him in a silent meal.

"I watched the scene next to me like an audience at an ancient play. I had heard it, overheard it, before. I recognized the body language. Women leaning forward, men sitting at a slight remove. Wives grinding the conversation in gear, husbands disengaging. Where are you going? Out. What are you thinking? Nothing.

"But what made it all so much more poignant this time was that this husband and wife were in their eighties. It was possible, I calculated, that for fifty years, for sixty years, she wanted to know what he was thinking. Wanted to reach into his mind and he had given her *nothing.*"

Her column strikes a tender spot in the lives of many

couples. A lazy insensitivity to the other makes one talk too little and the other too much. One seeks intimacy, the other avoids it or plays games with it. Of such stuff are marriages often made.

She takes silence as *disapproval*. He takes silence as *approval*. No wonder they nurse so many wounds. Can these two ever meet? Yes, if they will begin feeling responsible to not only talk to each other but to listen. David Seamonds, in his book *Putting Away Childish Things*, comments, "Isn't it incredible that a married couple can love each other, live together, make love to one another, bring up children together, yet never really communicate to one another what they are actually feeling?"[13] Look around and find it credible. Poor communication is the source of most marital unhappiness.

Communication problems do not begin with marriage; they are evident during courtship. They are simply ignored in the headiness of romantic involvement. Wisely someone has said that most courting couples need a lot more talking and a lot less heavy breathing. A marriage that evolves primarily from erotic attraction usually runs aground because the couple have never learned to talk together about what they are thinking and feeling.

It is a childish view that marriage does not require work or that love makes things happen automatically. Most marriages are not made in heaven; they come in kits, and you have to put them together yourselves. A good marriage requires the work of good communication whether we feel like it or not. It takes maturity to do the work. Immaturity plays silly games. "What's wrong?" The person clams up, instead of speaking up, and finally replies, "Oh, nothing," with the steam of anger hissing around the edges or the gloom of despair graying the atmosphere. *Guess what's wrong; I dare you!* Probably people who pout aren't old enough to get married, but some of us go on pouting into old age.

In such a heated climate talking often begins with an outpouring of negatives. Sometimes it is truth, but not truth spoken in love. Accusations cause defensive reactions. Communication goes nowhere. But even this faulty communication is better than no communication because understanding might come if both confront their feelings.

Confrontations are not always wrong; usually they mean someone cares how things are. Putting someone down is different from putting something right, and we need to distinguish between anger that destroys and anger that builds. Anger can be a great strength; its problem is that it is easily mixed with bitterness. The idea that good Christians never express their true feelings, especially negative ones, is nonsense. The ideal of the great stone-faced, highly controlled person is neither Christian nor human. Such a person may fit corporate headquarters, but husbands who do not cry have not blessed their marriages so much as impaired them.

Emotions are given to us by God, and intimacy means using our emotions to grow closer to each other. Conflict is often the price of growing intimacy because of the struggle to understand another person. Out of such conflict we learn better ways to communicate. Unless a couple begins talking and sharing about ordinary events and ideas and feelings, their talk about troubled situations will always be explosive. A commitment to communicate is basic. E. Stanley Jones once said that sometimes you have to feel yourself into a new way of acting, but other times you have to act yourself into a new way of feeling. Communication is a learned art, particularly in an emotional context. You have to do it; it is part of the work of a good marriage.

Everyone longs for intimacy. We may experience it in part in friendship, but it is experienced best in marriage. It comes with taking the risk to be transparent in the safety of your troth. It comes with a kind of openness to understand yourself and your own meanings. It is a kind of adventure in knowing another person. It means standing emotionally in the other person's shoes.

One night, as we lay in bed talking and not understanding each other, we began laughing at our impasse and turned the light back on to draw a diagram of what was happening in our conversation.

Person A was sharing her *feelings*. Person B chose to ignore these, hoping to go to sleep.

Person A continued talking, Person B talked back saying it was foolish to feel that way.

The solution came when B moved to be psychological-ly in tune with A so that his response was, "I understand; I care." Feeling understood would allow A to relax and listen to B's advice.

That may seem a simplistic way to solve a communication gap, but we have found repeatedly that the effort to understand what the other is saying emotionally draws us together. People say things differently. Hearing what is said is the important part. Only a listener who hears can speak accurately on the feeling level. It is the principle of answering an idea with an idea and a feeling with a feeling.

Yet looking at our marriage, it is praying together that has drawn us close to each other. Nothing is hidden from God; we are thoroughly known by our Heavenly Father. We dare not pretend before him. Confession is often our most appropriate response, if there has been tension. Forgiveness of each other is seen in the light of our need to be forgiven by God. "Be kind and compassionate to one another, forgiving each other, just as in Christ God forgave you" (Ephesians 4:32). Simply laying before him our dreams, disappointments, hurts, concerns, joys, and our family life—the long list of cares and thankful feelings we store up each day—is a way of uniting us and reminding us who is the real guardian of our marriage. We don't make long speeches to God, each with a proper introduction. We simply talk to God back and forth as things come to our minds. No preaching at each other; that is manipulation. Just honest conversation with God.

When prayer is a habit, a part of our daily routine, bringing our lives before God has a healing, humbling effect. When big hurts or misunderstandings tend to make one want to nurse a grievance, the habit of laying it before God means consciously letting God look at it. He gives a new perspective on what is really important as his forgiveness and our own sinfulness become apparent. Beyond this is the joy of thankfulness. Thankfulness keeps life in tune; it provides the ballast for the ship. Being thankful for the delights of life—

our grandson Austin's first step, fresh paint for the kitchen walls, the sunset—as well as our basic needs provides a climate in which intimacy thrives.

Prayer is an intimate experience, especially when two people pray alone. That is why we caution dating couples about praying alone with each other; it can give a sense of intimacy that may mislead one or the other to think the relationship is more serious than it really is. Wait until the commitment is definite, then begin. Prayer must not be used as a gimmick to provide a desired closeness. Prayer is talking to God and demands honesty in motive as well as words. Otherwise it is not prayer; it is a phony ritual.

It is the very intimacy of prayer that keeps some husbands and wives from praying together, even though each may have a personal prayer life. A kind of embarrassment or shyness before each other is like a sound barrier that needs to be broken to give both husband and wife the freedom to come together before God. Why two people who live so closely with each other should feel shy about talking to God together is a bit of a puzzle. We suspect it is a reality that goes back to Eden. The problem is overcome by a frank admission of fears followed by prayer. Begin by telling your feelings to God and ask for his help. He is known for his gracious compassion. If you think it will take a miracle, you will find that you have come to the right Source for whatever you need.

*Money.* Money is a second marital hazard. It sometimes relates to communication because it too is often hard to talk about. Family finances become a source of contention when two people have different ideas about how to use money. Either the husband is frustrated that he works so hard and his wife spends so carelessly that they never get ahead, or the frugal wife is appalled at her husband's extravagance for things they don't need. Money represents security to most people, and a threat to security does not lead to peace.

Quarreling about money does not restore either peace or security; practical communication is necessary to set up a budget. If a couple cannot manage to talk through a budget and make sensible commitments, they need to seek the professional family budgeting help available today. A solution from an objective source outside the marriage has merit if the couple cannot reach a compromise.

Credit cards sometimes make their users feel richer than they are, and cardholders end up poorer than they need to be. Credit cards may need to be destroyed if they cause a war every time household bills are paid. Communication here is crucial.

Trouble comes not only with shortage of money but with too much money and its careless stewardship. Both parents and children tend to lose their sense of values when money is easily available. Parents buy off their children; children exploit parents. And both lose their sense of surprise and thankfulness. Much of what we think *we must have* we could do without and be happier. We pamper our pride. We may even look down on the way someone else spends money and fail to see we are extravagant in areas where another person is frugal.

Our biggest money problem comes from thinking that all we have belongs to us—except perhaps our tithe. Ten percent for God and ninety percent for us. We may call that stewardship, but it is the opposite. Stewards act in behalf of a master who is the real owner. Stewardship recognizes that *all* we have belongs to God and asks him how much we need to live in the way he wants us to live. That may be different for each family. If Christian believers lived this way we would free up funds to feed the poor and establish long-range projects that would build the church around the world and meet social and economic needs as well. No one can outgive

God. Many of our sadnesses come from our own ungenerous spirits.

Money problems are one of the reasons wives have returned to the job market. Many of these are single parents who are trying to keep a family together and are its sole supporter. The high cost of housing and automobiles means that money doesn't stretch as far as it once did, and mothers of young children are finding jobs to help the family budget. For others, a career is basic in their lifestyle, both financially and emotionally; they never intended to be in the home continually.

Whatever the cause, stress comes to family life because of careers—whether it be the husband's or the wife's career. Family life needs care-givers, and when careers come before care-giving, relationships are caught in the middle. Nurturing our children, giving them values, and furnishing their minds with concepts and ideals should not be left to strangers or professionals. Mothers who have the option do themselves and their children a disservice if they don't give primary care for them during the earliest years of life. Children need quantity time as well as quality time.

Over half of all mothers with preschool children are now working full or part-time, which represents a dramatic change in family life since the early 1960s. Millions of children six years old and under are now in some type of child-care arrangement outside the home. Many more children come home to empty houses after school. The pressure is on. That means a change in the concept of home, not only for children but for husbands and wives as well. And it changes the world the woman lives in who opts to stay at home. Rather than following the crowd, married couples must take a realistic look at what they want in their commitment to each other.

Mothers are not the only care-givers in the family.

Husbands and fathers have been able to neglect both wife and children for the sake of a career and have done so with little rebuke from society. It has been the American way! Now that wives are pursuing careers—and some with the diligence of men—the damage careers can bring to a family becomes more obvious. Both husband and wife need to examine their priorities. What is really important in life? Is the extra money worth the stress on relationships? What will taking a promotion do to your family? How do you balance monetary rewards with spiritual values? Are other people outside the home more important than your own family? Is the stress you feel temporary or long-range?

Unless you value relationships you may use up all your days in pursuit of that which does not satisfy. In the end, you are only indispensable to those who love you best. Everywhere else you can quickly and easily be replaced. Such is the final picture that crystallizes in a life where money and careers are the only values. Some people learn that lesson too late.

## A Summing Up

Marriage is the highest commitment among humans of which man is capable. It is the most intense form of total-life commitment in its demand for mutuality and complementarity.[14] It is the only relationship in which we can experience the marvelous blend of loves—erotic, philia, and agape. Every husband and wife have within themselves not only the love that draws them together but also those things that would drive them apart. No wonder, then, that marriage is a relationship where growth is essential to its success.

Every couple has a choice about what they will make of their life together. Basically marriages seem to fall into three different categories. In one, each person goes a different way and does his own thing, and the strength of each is no greater than if they had not married. In a second category, each partner pulls the other down so that the marriage makes both less than they would be if they had not married. In the third category, two people build each other's strength so that each becomes more than they could be apart and their marriage is stronger than the sum of the two of them. At any point, a couple can begin to work on the third category.

Marriage is based on reality, not dreams. You take the stuff of life—strengths, weaknesses, hurts, distrust, poor communication skills—and build the relationship into something beautiful and durable. It is a possibility because of being created in the image of God, being called to belong to him, and being married in a union he himself designed when he gave the first bride away.

---

[1] R. David Freedman, "Woman, A Power Equal to Man," *Biblical Archaeology Review*, January/February 1983, 56. Dr. Freedman's area of study is Assyriology and Northwest Semitic languages. The translation of *ezer* as *helper* does not negate the idea of strength or partnership. A term that contains the same root word for helper is used of God himself. "God is my helper (here *azar*, the same root as *ezer*)." The offense of "a helper fit for him" comes from the interpretation given it over the years.

[2] Dwight Hervey Small, *Christian: Celebrate Your Sexuality* (Old Tappan, N.J.: Fleming H. Revell Co., 1974), 151.

[3] James Olthuis, *I Pledge You My Troth* (New York: Harper & Row, 1975), 21.

[4]Lewis Smedes, *Sex for Christians* (Grand Rapids: Wm. B. Eerdmans Publishing Co., 1976), 174.

[5]Ibid., 176.

[6]James Spickelmier, "Marriage is for Keeps," *The Standard* magazine, June 1983, 3.

[7]Walter Trobisch, *I Married You* (New York: Harper & Row, 1971), 79.

[8]Anne Morrow Lindbergh, *Gift from the Sea* (New York: Pantheon Books, 1955), 104.

[9]Olthuis, *I Pledge You My Troth*, 27.

[10]Smedes, *Sex for Christians*, 187.

[11]Olthuis, *I Pledge You My Troth*, 26.

[12]Ellen Goodman, "The Rejection of Intimacy," © 1979, The Boston Globe Newspaper Company/Washington Post Writers Group. Reprinted with permission.

[13]David Seamonds, *Putting Away Childish Things* (Wheaton, Ill.: Victor Books, 1983), 57.

[14]Small, *Christian: Celebrate Your Sexuality*, 176.

*chapter* 8

# The Family Of God

Christians are forgiven sinners. The church is the only group you join by admitting how bad you are and how much you need a Savior. Only people who understand that they fall short of God's standard can come to Christ to be forgiven and reconciled to God. That is what a Christian is: a forgiven, reconciled sinner, someone with a new loyalty and a new life—but still a forgiven sinner.

That is worth repeating, because the church sometimes gets into trouble by forgetting it, and such forgetfulness leads its members to pretense, disdain, or hiding instead of honest association with each other. Jesus himself said he came to call sinners, not the righteous, to repentance.

The decision to become a Christian is a personal one, but it is not a private one. As soon as a person comes to Christ and becomes one of his, that person finds himself part of a family—the family of God. He may not always like the brothers and sisters in this family, but that doesn't matter; he didn't choose them. God did. None of us got to choose our natural family either. The privilege of being part of the family is what matters.

## What the Church Is

We need to be reminded that the church is the family of God. It is not a collection of perfect people wearing haloes who never make mistakes and have no sharp edges. Instead it is a gathering of clay pots, each of which contains a treasure (2 Corinthians 4:7). Some are more comely than others; they have a finer finish or a better shape. None of them belongs because of its exterior, but rather, for the treasure inside.

A comparison should never be made between the nice non-Christian and the not-so-nice Christian. That is like comparing peaches with pears. But we can compare what a person was before he accepted Christ with what he is and *is becoming* since his conversion. Some people are "nice" simply because of a good digestive system and proper training. That is why when such a person becomes a Christian, one might say, "But you've always been a Christian," equating a nice exterior with a redeemed interior. This only shows how little we understand what it means to belong to Christ and on what basis one can relate to a Holy God. A nice exterior just won't do it.

That is not to say that those who belong to God's family won't begin to be more and more like their Father as time goes on. If you spend time with him, you do become like him, because God is in the process of bringing many children to glory who bear the likeness of Jesus Christ. That is the work the Holy Spirit proposes to do in believers. It is a process of growth, and the ones to worry about are not the problem cases where so much growth *needs* to take place, but the self-satisfied ones who haven't shown a sign of growth for years. In one sense, heaven is not reached in a single bound. And God expects his children to actively participate in their Christian growth. In another sense, heaven *is* reached in a single bound—the moment a person believes and receives Christ, his hope of heaven is a sure thing.

*Attitudes within the church*

The climate within God's family, the church, should encourage growth. The brothers and sisters within the family are concerned about understanding and becoming more like Christ. They support one another. That is why we need to commit ourselves to a group of believers in a local church. His plan is to use one clay pot in the life of another clay pot, to underscore the importance of their interior treasures, and to show that "this all-surpassing power is from God and not from us" (2 Corinthians 4:7). The church was never meant to be a place that one attends like a concert and leaves unknown and untouched when the music is over.

There is a sense in which the church is a universal, invisible collection of believers in all ages. However, the universal application of the word "ecclesia" (church) represents less than ten percent of its usage in Scripture.[1] Almost every other biblical reference to "church" is to a local, face-to-face gathering of God's family, his church.

Therefore, God's family meets together to encourage its members to grow into the Father's likeness—which is what the godly life is all about. Family members need teaching;

they must learn how to think like Christians so they can begin to act like Christians. They need the deep nourishment of corporate worship to focus on God, his grace, and his mercy. They will sing their theology, and the overflow of their thankful hearts will be like a sweet fragrance going up before God. They will rehearse the marvelous acts of God and come before his throne with the expectation that he will again act in the affairs of men.

It is only natural to expect that the family members would love God, the triune God. After all, he has provided everything they need for "life and godliness"(2 Peter 1:3), and he has poured out his love upon all the members of his family. They know there is no hope in this life or the next without him. His Word matters to the family members. Their meat and drink is to hear a word from the Triune God and then to obey him. To know God is to know that our obedience is due him.[2] It makes sense to love, listen, and obey, but in actual practice some of the family members are often in trouble because they do not do these very things.

The Father of this family is also a King. He is building a kingdom, enlarging it, and taking over territory from the Enemy. And his subjects are granted the privilege of participation in what the King is doing. These are not soldiers on white chargers; they are simple people like us who rehearse to others what God has done. Some of the best kingdom-builders are hardly noticed because they are simply faithful in serving and doing what the King wants. Others are prophets or teachers or public proclaimers. Some have gifts of helping. But the King himself must be the focus of all they do or say if they are building his kingdom and not their own.

It is the business of the church to build the kingdom of God. The church is people—not buildings and super-organizations. The kingdom of God is a spiritual kingdom made up of people who own him as king and who are God's willing subjects. It may be defined as local or universal, militant or triumphant, but regardless of how it is defined, the basic element of the church is *people* who belong to his kingdom. The children's song is true:

> The church is not a building,
> The church is not a steeple,
> The church is not a resting place,
> The church is the people.

And it is a people who are loved by God. That is the shocking thing, because we can hardly believe it sometimes when we look at the church. At one time we were in a very troubled church, which was full of discord and sinners who had forgotten they had been forgiven and were thus unforgiving. One morning a guest speaker, who knew little about the church, startled everyone by saying, "The Lord loves his church. He gave himself for it. The Lord loves *this* church. He died for all its members." People glanced furtively around the congregation. The Lord loves this church? These people? Oh, yes, he loves me. But these other rebellious sinners?

There's the rub. Sometimes it is hard to tell whether the church *is* the church. And what about family members loving God and His Word? What about spiritual growth and godliness? Some members don't seem to bear much family resemblance, or are they in the family like rebellious teenagers? Are they simply clay pots who have forgotten that they hold a treasure? That is the problem with the church: It isn't ideal; it is made up of sinners.

*Leadership in the church*

Many unbiblical ideas of church leadership are in operation all around us. Some churches operate on the corporate model, the structure patterned according to American business methods. But the church is the family of God. It needs leadership and organization, but it is not judged by the success pattern of the corporation—not biblically at least. The church is more a living organism than an organization. When big business sits on the church board, it needs to be aware of what the church is and what it isn't.

In other places church leaders act like kings and treat the people as subjects. They forget that we have but one King, Jesus. A significant thing about the real King is that his leadership is that of a servant. In the family of God, the members are expected to function as full members who know and understand, who grow and respond. Irresponsible people always want someone else to be spiritual for them. God insists that everyone in his family grow up and be personally accountable. That is what makes the gulf between clergy and laity—a gulf encouraged by some systems—so disastrous. It promotes a two-class system or a layered hierarchy with decreasing spirituality *expected* on the lower rungs of the ladder. People are ready to follow this kind of leadership because it relieves them of the responsibility. Let the "professionals" build the kingdom!

The solution is not to opt for a leaderless church. Such a thing would not exist; indeed it would never begin. The church uses organization even if it is not essentially an organization, just as a family uses organization to operate. But the biblical description of the church does not give organizational details. Look at the terms that define the church: the family of God, the body of Christ, the people of God, the flock of God. They are relational not organizational.

Many different organizational forms may properly fall within biblical guidelines, but Scripture is strangely silent about a specific structure for the church.

### The purpose of the church

What, then, is the purpose of the church as the family of God? It is fellowship and mission. *Koinonia* is the fellowship of the family that produces spiritual growth in its members, and mission is the building of the kingdom of God by making what is true about God and his standards known to others. The job of the church is to be concerned about what God is concerned about.

The working out of the purposes of the church is complicated by our self-centeredness. We can get more concerned about whether the sanctuary has a middle aisle for weddings than whether the church is fulfilling its purpose in the sight of God. We slip into organizational solutions and structures to solve our problems instead of expecting God to change attitudes. We measure success in terms of size, budget, and political influence. Howard Snyder comments that the church gets into trouble whenever it thinks it is in the church business instead of the kingdom business.[3] It is easier to have more committee meetings than to pray. Indeed much of our church work is not the work of the church at all.

Local churches differ from each other in reflecting the purposes. Each group of believers has a certain "flavor," as God honors the individuality of his children. When there is only one "believing church" in town, then those who belong to God's family will be part of that. The luxury of choice does not exist, and it is significant that whenever pressure mounts against believers, their family-ness becomes more important than the nonessentials of *how* things are done. Think of all the places in the world throughout the centuries where small groups of believers have gathered in secret in a home or a field—glad to be together, encouraging each other and worshiping God. That is the church, the family of God.

The difference in congregations is often cultural and involves elements of worship and form. Churches also differ on certain theological issues—baptism, the Lord's supper, pacifism, and so forth—but if the church is truly the church, the basic body of Christian truth must be upheld, preached, and practiced. Theology *is* important! Believers indwelt by the Holy Spirit have discernment. They know the difference between "bread" and "a stone" whether there are stained-glass windows in the church or not. Among church bodies that are truly Christian, genuine fellowship should exist. We dare not make God's love too narrow or exclusive by "false limits of our own." Relating within the church is complicated by the diversity within it, but that diversity is also its enrichment. Sameness and unity are not synonyms.

### Decision making in the church

We've talked so much about unity and peace, according to Lynn Buzzard, Director of Christian Conciliation Service, that we haven't developed an adequate theology of conflict. Not all conflict is bad. What is bad is not knowing how to handle it. Tension comes with differences of opinion, and since we are not carbon copies of each other in our disposition or training, we are bound to disagree.

Decision making in the church is almost sure to bring disagreement. Probably few conflicts arise out of koinonia, or fellowship. The relational troubles come when the church members begin to make decisions about their mission, even if the mission is only the size of the church parking lot.

"The church is not just about sweetness," says Buzzard. "It

is in fact about power, choices, competing values, self interests, noble ideals, anger and all the rest.... If the church is moving *toward* something, then there's going to be debate about what that something is and how we get there and who's going to lead us."

Conflict makes people nervous, particularly in the church. We keep remembering that Christ prayed we would be one. Love for one another is to be our hallmark and oneness is part of love. But facing conflict honestly may be the best way to learn how to love and become one. The wonder of the church is the way "unity emerges from separation, differentness, the alien and stranger being brought into citizenship in the kingdom of God.... Unity becomes precious when you walk through conflict in order to reach it."[4]

Dissenting opinions need not lead to dissension. Usually there are at least two ways to look at anything, and we need to learn how to hear each other out. By listening to each other and being honest about our thoughts *we can* clarify the issue for every one and lead to increased understanding and unity. It cuts the throat of the kind of politicking and masking of the issues that often takes place when conflict must be avoided at all costs.

All of us need to learn how to do this without causing dissension. Insecurity prompts deep emotions that often lead to hostility against a brother or sister and makes one suspicious of others and even paranoid. You line up people to be on your side, for example. You "talk about the issue" with your friends, but the other person "gossips" about you. It is all in your point of view.

We take our built-in prejudices and try to pass off our view as God's view. We use spiritual jargon and prayer as weapons against another person, but we often avoid setting up a situation where we really listen to each other. Our "righteous indignation" is scarcely ever biblically merited.

It is not easy to be human together, but it is important in the decision-making process to recognize our common humanity. If we could look at our differences as a sharpening tool to arrive at the best decision instead of as a personal spat, we would eliminate much of the relational hassle that takes place in the church. Maybe God's will—what would really please him—would be to see people willingly give way on one of their pet ideas and enthusiastically support the larger group's decision. We assume, of course, that the hassle is not over something basic to Christian truth.

Troubled relationships also involve personality clashes— the kind of thing that can happen in any family. Clay pots jostle each other on the shelf. Sometimes it is because we don't really know each other. Irritating ways remind us of something in our past. When Joe Smith gets up each year to voice his objections to the church budget he sounds just like old Mr. Flanigan from the church you grew up in. And the way Pete Sanders always has people sing the first and last verses at the evening service reminds you of cultural ways you left behind years ago! That is when it is good to remember that you may affect someone else the same way.

All of us entered a climate of acceptance and forgiveness when we came to Christ. It is the very air we breathe in the church. We need to breathe that air more deeply and share it with our brothers and sisters in God's family. "Accept one another, then, just as Christ accepted you, in order to bring praise to God"(Romans 15:7). The effusion of God's love and acceptance is sufficient for all clay pots.

## Pity the Preacher

One of the sorest points in church life is conflict over the minister. Few churches have a decent way to handle pastoral relationships, and ministers aren't always adept at facing their accusers. Who wants to be criticized or lose a job, particularly when getting another post means uprooting the family and moving to a new locale? Sometimes a minister wants to organize his supporters and push out the dissidents. On occasion he takes his supporters and forms a new church. Such action always involves his pride, his self-view, or his future.

On the other hand, there are the unhappy church members. How do they suggest the minister leave? Often the one least equipped to be the cool spokesman presents their case. It comes off hostile, but at least it is out in the open. People are embarrassed to talk it over with the minister; instead, they talk about it with other people. The minister is increasingly uncertain about who is "against him." Everything was once so rosy. What happened?

It is hard to handle liking the minister's family as people while still feeling it may be time for them to leave. Some people protest by leaving the church; it is their way of saying how they feel. Others withhold funds to get the message across. People who don't like trouble, who get knots in their stomachs over tensions, stay away from everyone and try not to have an opinion.

To write that these things happen in the church is painful because it is the surest way to spoil both fellowship and a sense of mission, and it gives the impression that the Holy Spirit is out of business. Accusations sometimes become irrational; suspicions grow. That is not good. We must not hurt brothers and sisters that way. "Whatever you did for one of the least of these brothers of mine, you did it for me," says the Lord of the church (Matthew 25:40).

But we are clay pots—earthen vessels—and sometimes it is necessary for a minister to be asked to leave. In itself that is not bad. It could be the means for growth for everyone involved if attitudes and behavior line up with biblical principle. And we would grow if we believed the Lord of the church could do something to help and would do it on his timetable, not ours. We find it very hard to trust God when we are uncomfortable.

In addition, other leaders in the church need to direct the way with spiritual wisdom that takes the risk of confronting both minister and people. Most relationship problems in the church narrow down to one question: Who will be spiritual and wise?

Our human inclination is to be either so truthful that graciousness is lacking or so gracious that we are not truthful. Our feeling-oriented culture rarely opts for the harshness of truth today. Compassion almost leads people to feel sympathy for the devil. Sin seemingly cannot be separated from the sinner; so we are gracious even to sin. What results is a weak, flabby kind of emotion falsely labeled love.

The church, if it is to be the church, must call its members to accountability before God and Scripture. The Gospel writer John said that Jesus Christ was full of "grace and truth" (John 1:14). We need both of those qualities in our lives if we are to evaluate ourselves and others in the church.

## Discipline in the Church

Discipline in the family of God, the church, is not a popular subject. Whenever it is discussed someone inevitably brings up a horror story from the past that rivals *The Scarlet Letter*. The necessity of discipline in the church today is dangerously unclear, which is why it is ignored by most bodies of believers. Yet we have not asked the basic question: Is God being honored? Has ignoring discipline helped either the church as a whole or the person in violation of God's standards? Is our goal to make a willful sinner feel comfortable in the church when only repentant sinners should feel comfortable in the family?

"It is unthinkable that the kingdom of God should tolerate within its fellowship unrepentant sin, open rebellion. That belongs to the kingdom of this world," writes Ben Patterson, pastor of Irvine Presbyterian Church in California. "Calling the church the kingdom of God also means that the church is ultimately a theocracy, not a democracy. It is ruled by a Lord. . . . In the church there can be but one authority, and that is the Lord. And there can be but one response from those in the church, and that is obedience. As fellow members, we have the right to expect of one another obedience to the Lord. There is a crisis in the church whenever the leaders are not willing to discipline members who are willfully and unrepentantly disobeying the Lord."[5]

Patterson goes on to say that there is also a crisis in "followership" in our churches—a profound resistance to being led and therefore being disciplined. Our individual needs and desires become our final authority. We choose leaders, then, whom we can identify with rather than those who have a prophetic word for us.

Our mobility and the impersonal nature of the city hinders the effectiveness of discipline. In a small community a person would be well-known. In the city, a person under discipline in one church can join a church down the street where no one asks any questions about either his past or present. We are sufficiently fragmented denominationally to have no inter-church communication. This is used as an argument against church discipline with the implication that it doesn't do any good anyway. But that may simply be cultural accommodation.

Others are reluctant about discipline because certain social sins are targeted rather than the complete biblical list of sins. And who wants to say they are sinless and cast the first stone? the dissenters ask, remembering Jesus and the woman taken in adultery. In discussions about the issue, someone often will mention a character he knew like the elder who directed the discipline of a wayward person and at the same time was misusing a client's savings. But no one knew about that.

All of this is interesting, but it doesn't answer the basic questions about church family discipline. Certain principles emerge, however. First, for discipline to be effective, the fellowship of the body must be of such a quality—so sweet and so good—that its absence would be sorely missed. To be excluded would mean to be cut off from your family.

Second, that repentance is encouraged by the love of the church family; they are more caring than censorious.

Third, the point of the discipline is restoration, the reconciliation of the erring one first to God, then to the church family. Fourth, discipline reminds people of the church family standards.

Every one of these principles applies in the natural family. The point of discipline is always "the peaceful fruit of righteousness" and an enhancing of relationships. According to the Scripture, discipline is a positive, affirming action. It produces disciples.

Discipline is a sensitive issue. We have no flawless policy to offer. But we do know this: If the church is to do the work of the church, it must *be* the church. A concern for holiness, for the greater glory of God, is never amiss, and although the church may make mistakes in discipline as it learns how to do it, it will make no greater mistake than doing nothing at all.

Church leadership cannot produce the perfect church any more than parents can produce perfect children, but they can be godly and take a stand for godly behavior. They must warn and teach and counsel. Some will be grateful, reminded of truth, and restored to their senses. Others may refuse to be led or disciplined, but careful, godly wisdom will prove itself with the passage of time.

A special responsibility is laid on church leadership to maintain the purity of the church. Paul's strong words in 1 Corinthians 5 about dealing with immorality in the church cannot be relegated solely to another culture. Applying that passage is admittedly complicated, but the Word of God needs to be taken seriously. Just before his instruction to expel the immoral brother, Paul declared, "For the kingdom of God is not a matter of talk but of power" (1 Corinthians 4:20). We hear a lot of talk in today's church, but where is the power?

We solve relational problems in the church the same way all people-problems are solved—by open confrontation, discussion, and forgiveness. In Matthew 18 Jesus gives careful instruction about the way to resolve the problem of "your brother sinning against you." First go and talk, just the two of you. If he listens, you have won your brother over. If he doesn't listen, take one or two along. Then if he still refuses to listen, take the matter to the church.

That seems to imply that everyone does not need to know everything about every personal sin. What Jesus taught is a way to keep short accounts, to handle sin, to keep communications clear, to live transparently. The pattern seems appropriate for church discipline in general. It is a paradigm for all human relationships.

## A Final Reminder

Our Father is remarkably careful about his children. When we are born the first time, we are placed in the care of a human family—father, mother, brothers, sisters, aunts, uncles. They nurtured, disciplined and trained us for many years. They provided the world in which we developed as human beings. We will never really outgrow our natural family connections.

When we are born the second time—made spiritually alive—our heavenly Father places us in a spiritual family. It is *his* family in a special way, the family of God. The members of that body—the fathers, mothers, brothers, sisters, aunts, and uncles—and their variety of personalities and gifts surround us with God's love. They provide the climate for our spiritual development—the nurture, discipline, and training we need until we mature as believers.

Every one in this second family is a believer, a saint. It is a big family; it goes beyond the local church and extends to ages past and ages still to come.

Each year some go on ahead to a place in heaven prepared just for them. Each year the train is longer. The saints militant, fighting in the battles of this world, and the saints triumphant above, praising God and cheering us on like spectators in the arena—that is the church. We must never lose sight of the glory of being part of it.

> O blest communion, fellowship divine!
> We feebly struggle, they in glory shine;
> Yet all are one in Thee, for all are Thing.
> Alleluia![6]

[1]Robert Young, *Analytical Concordance to the Bible* (New York: Funk and Wagnalls, 1936), 176.

[2]C. S. Lewis, *Surprised By Joy* (New York: Macmillan Company), chapter 15.

[3]Howard Snyder, *Liberating the Church* (Downers Grove, Ill.: InterVarsity Press, 1983), 11.

[4]Lynn Buzzard, "War and Peace in the Local Church," *Leadership Magazine* (Summer 1983), 22.

[5]Ben Patterson, "Discipline, the Backbone of the Church," *Leadership Magazine*, (Winter 1983), 108.

[6]William Walsham How, "For All the Saints," *Hymns* II (Downers Grove, Ill.: InterVarsity Press, 1976), 159.

# Frustrated Relationships

Troubled relationships do not end when someone says, "Let's split." Only rocks split; people tear. Spoiled relationships cause most of the pain in life. It *is* true that we live outside of Eden; all of us know that. The tearing of relationships, whether in life or death, is a grim reminder that we live in a fallen world. We are imperfect people, clay pots jostling against each other. We don't like hurting, but hurting is as real as sin. We are selfish; we make wrong choices. We *blame* others for our pain; we *bring* pain to others. The presence of sin in the world erupts in unexpected ways—disease, accidents, the taking of life. Untimely death

207

sometimes shortens the best of relationships. Life doesn't always go according to dreams, and frustration is our common lot.

This book has explored what relationships can be. Even though they are not always as we described, that does not invalidate their potential. Giving and forgiving relationships are possible, which is a fact that needs to be emphasized. As damaged relationships multiply in the world at large, it seems easier to lower the standard, to accept less, to expect less, to be satisfied with lowest-common-denominator living. Realizing the potential of relationships means knowing what the standard is and what life's good possibilities are so that our own willfulness does not lead us astray. The pain we feel over broken relationships tells us that we were made for more than we sometimes realize.

From time to time, a woman who recently immigrated to the United States tells us vignettes of her childhood that inevitably bring tears to our eyes. Her story seems like one long tale of sadness and deprivation of love. Recently she asked, "How is it that you who have known none of these things weep the most for me?"

We thought for a moment and then replied, "It's because we have been loved and cared for that we know what family life can be—and *we* know what you have missed!" Knowing how it could be makes all the difference in our appreciation of relationships.

This chapter is about *hurting*. We struggled to find one word that would describe the wide range of torn relationships people experience. We settled on *frustrated* after looking up its meaning in the dictionary:

Frustrate, v.t.:     *to come between a person and his aim or desire or to defeat another's plan*; ant. *fulfill*.

Frustrated, adj.: *feeling deep insecurity, discouragement or dissatisfaction in some endeavor or purpose.*

It may not contain an adequate feeling of pain, but otherwise its meaning indicates that what is hoped for is not what is experienced. Frustration in a relationship can take many forms: the frustration that comes from 1) unfulfilled connections, wanting a relationship that already exists to be more than it is; 2) conflict, quarreling that unsettles and threatens to break people apart; 3) a marriage in trouble; 4) divorce, the rejection of a life once shared and the breaking of promises; 5) death; 6) other complexities.

## 1. Unfulfilled Connections

Frustration over unfulfilled connections most often occurs within families. A natural connection already exists, but sometimes it simply is not fulfilling. This mis-connection could be a son who has desired approval and an open show of love from his father for many years and yet has received only criticism. He feels like he never has measured up in his father's eyes, and a wound begins to eat away at his insides. It affects his emotional life, his sense of direction. He can't seem to be rid of the bitterness deep inside even though he manages to get on with life, marry, and begin a career.

Eventually he has a child of his own and watches as his father becomes to that grandchild what he never was to him—the affirming, loving person he longed for. He finds himself jealous of his own child as he pushes down years of resentment. A deep and good relationship has been denied him; he feels starved for some kind of basic fatherly approval. He sees his son sitting on the lap he does not remember ever sitting on and being hugged in a way he was never hugged.

He talks to his father about it, but the father doesn't understand. In desperation he pours out the anger and bitterness he has been storing up. His father suggests he stop talking nonsense and grow up. Is frustration a strong enough word to define such hurt? How does a person cope with that kind of unfulfilled relationship?

We'd like to think the father later thought it over and wrote a letter to his son as a tangible piece of evidence that he loved and admired the kind of man the son had become. But often that does not happen.

Change the situation. Make it a daughter who still smarts under the comparisons her mother makes in which she always comes out the loser. She longs for a caring mother to comfort her when she hurts, but instead, she keeps getting more wounded by her mother's words. She spends years working through a view of herself as an adequate person, painful years of confusion that keep her from enjoying the good relationships she already has. She feels angry that her mother can still hurt her so deeply.

The story could easily be a parent's longing to relate to an apathetic son who takes his inheritance and "goes off into a far country" emotionally, making himself totally insensitive to the needs and longings of his parents. They reach out and are wounded for their trouble. When they held that little boy, loved him, and nourished him, they never dreamed it would turn out this way. What happened to his heart? How can he be so indifferent to relationships that were once so intimate? Every time they think of him they experience a terrible emptiness.

A friend of ours has a brother, her only relative, who never initiates contact with her even though he lives nearby. He responds to her in a polite and decent way, but nothing more. She often cries over that relationship because she wants it to be more. She is frustrated.

Usually the people who can hurt you most are people related to you either by birth or marriage. Because they are on your family tree, you expect some comfort from them. Instead, they say all the wrong things at the wrong time and do not apologize even though you dissolve in tears. You think it is their problem, and they think it is yours. You get the feeling they are blind to who you really are, as if they were relating to a stereotype. You try to level with them by revealing your heart, and that leaves you twice as vulnerable because they can't hear your pain; they are emotionally deaf. You want more than this—and your expectations make almost every encounter a nightmare. They keep surprising you with their indifference and lack of tact, as if they were trying to misunderstand.

Joyce Landorf calls these "irregular people" and has written a book about them.[1] You can't reason with them, depend on them, expect any real support from them; they don't act, react, speak, think, or even write the way we expect them to; these people belong to us and yet they hurt us. Landorf gets her phrase from a powerful screenplay taken from the book *Summer of My German Soldier*,[2] in which a cruel father pours out the wrath he accumulated from his own childhood onto his already wounded daughter, Patty. He is more unkind and terrible than any human ought to be to another. Shattered by what he said, Patty leaves home seeking a safe place. She finds her way to Ruth, a comforting black woman who used to work for their family. Holding her and listening to the tale, Ruth finally says to Patty, "Now here . . . when I go shopping and I see something marked 'irregular,' I know that I ain't gonna have to pay so much for it. Girl, you got yourself some irregular folks, and you've been paying top dollar for them all along. So just don't go wastin' up your life wishin' for what ain't gonna be!"

Paying "top dollar" emotionally for a relationship that "may never be" is poor stewardship; it means having less to spend on other relationships that may be more nourishing. That does not mean "writing them off" or ignoring the people involved; you will pay something no matter what you do. It does mean being realistic about the relationship and getting some perspective on it. Perfectionists sometimes fuss so much over what is not "just right" that they spoil what happiness they already have. We can't demand that anyone meet our felt needs; we can only be grateful if they do. To insist that someone be what they may be incapable of being is to insist on a kind of perfection not found in this life. Some things have to be let go and placed in God's hands. In the Lord's goodness, when one person fails us another often takes us up. He is not unaware of our needs.

The phrase "irregular people" seems nicely descriptive, but the truth is that since Adam, all of us are irregular in one way or another. Some have been pushed out of shape by their own experiences; faulty defense mechanisms callous their sensitivity. Others seem to be born with sharp corners that stick into people. Compassion for these sharp-cornered people may be more appropriate than anger. Yet feeling emotionally needy makes it hard to stand in another's shoes. Expectations get in the way of seeing where another person has been in the past.

A purging kind of confrontation with such people rarely helps; it only hurts the other person. It may provide ventilation for your built-up anger, but if the other person has not "heard" all these years, he or she will have no place for the large load you intend to dump. No matter that psychiatrists and counselors sometimes prescribe this as therapy for their patients; it is simply returning insensitivity for insensitivity. Most people are not intentionally cruel; they are just unaware. It is better to dump the load elsewhere and resist the temptation to tell someone off.

At some time in life someone else has not been faithful to the insensitive person—either by not loving or by not giving insights that could help. Maybe one of those unfaithful people has been *you*, probably because you didn't know how. Some people are unbelievably twisted; others simply interpret life in a different way. In any event, a life's accumulation of "wrongs" poured over another person is always destructive. You may tend to think that the person deserves it, but such expressions give some evidence of your having caught his "disease." The Holy Spirit is the one who illuminates the hearts and minds of people and convicts of wrongs.

Let your confrontation be gentle. Years of wrong can only be taken care of by forgiveness. We need to be humble about the realities of our blaming. You cannot live your life over again and neither can anyone else; we have to build on the good that already exists. What is past is past, and what is hurtful needs to be forgiven. *As God has been to me, so I must be to others.*

"Who cares about the past," you may think, "I only want the present and the future to be different." First you have to evaluate the past to permit you to act freely in the present. It is most likely that the person on your family tree who gives you the most problems has never experienced what you long for. That may be exactly where you can begin.

Watching our friend Sarah be creative in relating to her mother has been like seeing wisdom in action. Sarah wants a closer relationship with her parents, especially with her mother who seems so unfeeling toward her. She used to want love so desperately that everything she did turned out wrong. She set herself up to be hurt. She is wiser now, but she still would like some "mothering" even though she is married to a good man and has four children. Sarah doesn't doubt that her mother loves her; it is that her mother seems so unfeeling and unconcerned, as if she did her duty to get Sarah grown. And now that that is done, what more is there to ask for? What Sarah would like to ask for is some concern for her well-being, for her children, for her hurts—a healthy kind of loving that comes from *knowing* each other.

Instead, her parents have taken their considerable possessions and relocated two thousand miles away. They are not often heard from, and even then they do not show much concern for Sarah's family. After Sarah thought about her feelings of rejection and bitterness at being treated like an acquaintance by her mother, she decided to take the initiative and make something for her parents that was clearly an investment of her time and self. In between family and a part-time job she crocheted an afghan, which, in the end, turned out better than she had hoped; it was beautiful. She happily sent it off as a Christmas gift. No word came in return. Weeks later, in a telephone conversation, Sarah had to ask about the afghan. *Had they received it?* Yes, the package came before Christmas. Did she like it? asked Sarah.

"Yes, but we already had one," her mother responded.

Sarah was crushed, but she had the good sense to eventually see that she had made the afghan—not for them—but for herself. She had sent it with strings attached; she needed their affirmation. She had again set herself up to be hurt. Relating to her mother has been a series of advances and retreats. But Sarah saw it was wrong to do something with the idea of changing another person. Sarah needed to change her own behavior. She made a decision to *be* a warm, loving, giving person and to act like that kind of person. She had been letting her mother's behavior and reaction dictate how she was going to act and be. Sarah said, "I guess it has evolved over the years as I've forgiven her and had more compassion for the emptiness of her experience in life. I found myself wanting to enlarge her life a bit just by loving her."

Although Sarah had not outgrown her need for her mother, she could be more realistic about who her mother was and the extent of her emotional capabilities. Her mother was needy, too. By this time, God's kind of love—that "in spite of" love—showed her that she must follow her Heavenly Father's example. Sarah wired flowers to her parents on her own fortieth birthday with a note thanking them for all they had done for her. It wasn't phony. They had cared for her, provided for her as she grew up, and helped her in her education. The more she thought about it, the more Sarah felt the need to be thankful.

That action prompted an immediate call from her parents revealing their pleasure. Sarah said, "I really do love you both," and heard for the first time she could remember, "We love you, too"—from both voices at the other end of the line. She felt like she had finally grown up and made some progress in meeting her parent's emotional needs instead of lamenting over her own. Since that time many small miracles have happened, not the big ones Sarah still hopes for, but satisfying small things. Small gifts have arrived for no special day or reason, and more letters, as if something had been awakened. Sarah has put her demands of love aside and is happily enjoying the pleasure of new light on a horizon where she thought the sun would never rise.

Most people give up on relationships too soon. They don't like the discomfort and hurt, so they remove themselves quickly from the arena of pain or pretend everything is all right when it isn't. We have to learn how to make our interaction with others and our mutual dependency work. It is impossible to go through life without fender-benders along the way, and people who retreat from relationships miss the refinement and growth that comes from working things out. Working out our differences alleviates pain and guilt. Even if the person who hurts you never changes, you can change by growing into a more understanding and loving person. Otherwise we have two choices: either to be hurt at the whim of another person or to hide from important connections.

Some people prefer to avoid all confrontations. They fear how the other person will react or have a sense of inadequacy about the situation. But confrontations can be a way of saying, "I care." They are part of human dialogue, although they must be appropriate. We have learned that it is best to confront an issue at the time the event occurs instead of accumulating wrongs over a period of time. The discussion needs to be private, and the temptation to gather group support should be resisted. Love means mentioning the problem in the best possible context. Making a person feel like a total failure is not the purpose of the confrontation; nor is "getting even" the goal, nor is "straightening out" the behavior of another person. Confrontation, at its best, helps relationships, instead of spoiling them. It must help all principals in the discussion.

So then we must ask, What do I want to have happen as a result of confrontation? And we need to answer that very carefully. What can the person hear? How can they best hear what I have to say? Is what I intend to say accurate, or will I use the confrontation as a dumping ground for personal frustration? Am I being critical or is the confrontation intended for the good of both of us? Confrontation calls both partners to accountability.

A sense of humor and a light touch helps. Humor is

different from sarcasm. Sarcastic remarks usually put someone down, spill out of anger, and have an intentional barb. An undertone of anger makes everyone apprehensive and generally spoils communication.

## 2. Conflict and Quarrels

Confrontation is an emotional word. For some it is synonymous with quarreling. The mental image of a confrontational person is someone with sharp edges who challenges everything another says, insists on definitions (*what do you mean by that?*), and is hard to get along with. But confrontation can also be described as *care-fronting*. David Augsburger describes it this way: "Care-fronting has a unique view of conflict. Conflict is natural, normal, neutral and sometimes even delightful. It can turn into painful or disastrous ends, but it doesn't need to. Conflict is neither good nor bad, right nor wrong. Conflict simply is. How we view, approach and work through our differences does—to a large extent—determine our whole life pattern."[3]

Augsburger discusses the different ways people view conflict: 1) a given, a matter of fate, "we just can't get along"; 2) crushing, a rejection; 3) an issue of right and wrong; 4) mutual difference involving compromise and mediation; or 5) natural, neutral, normal. Usually a combination of these characterizes our view of conflict. The last option is the most freeing, leads most quickly to care-fronting, and involves love and truth in a neutral climate.

Most of us wish that conflict in any form would just disappear and seem surprised when it doesn't. We give it spiritual and moral value (*Good Christians shouldn't have these problems*) and thus deny both the uniqueness of the individuals involved and our common sinfulness. A sharper view of reality will help solve some of our problems.

This section zeros in on conflicts that involve those outside the family: quarrelsome neighbors, job conflicts, disagreements with acquaintances on politics or religion, and other misunderstandings that come between people. Any one of them can cause tightness in your stomach and tension at the back of your neck. You like peace, and now you have a neighbor who quarrels about everything: the way your kids slam the car doors, where your trash can sits, how often you mow the lawn, and especially the way your children behave. No other neighbor has ever complained. You feel under attack. Coming into your own driveway isn't the pleasure it used to be.

Or maybe it is the other way around. Your neighbor is a divorcee who doesn't like yard work. Her lawn is full of weeds and overgrown grass. Her weeds creep into your grass. You are embarrassed by her unsightly property and wish she would move into an apartment. When you see her out sunning or going golfing, your inner temperature rises.

Job conflicts probably account for most of the stress people feel. Some of the more common collisions include poor communication, organizational politics, the irritation of a colleague's performance, having your reputation undercut or your motives impugned, and holding to a difference of opinion about how things ought to be done. There is the management/union conflict, each with its own point of view about what is fair. Sometimes you feel that others take advantage of you, that work loads are not just, and that you resent the demeanor of your employer or an employee. Any of these is enough to cause irritation and conflict.

Some people are touchy, easily offended and critical of others. Their self-view makes it easily for them to assume negative motives on the part of another. Believing the best about another doesn't come easy to some people. Threatened people do not perceive truth accurately. They hear things that have not been said.

People are born with a variety of personality traits, which make some struggle more than others. Perfectionists, for example, often experience conflict in relationships. They disappoint themselves and set up standards for others that lead to further disappointment. They may find it hard to let other people be who they are and at the same time feel secure about themselves. They like to control details and may lack flexibility. Life has to line up the way they think it should and they are likely to distrust anyone who is spontaneous. Perfectionists tend to be anxious people who take life very seriously and sometimes make it too serious for others. They feel conflict and help create it.

Sometimes the differences have a theological basis. What you believe about God gives you a certain point of view. It tempers the decisions you might make. The use of the environment, for example, has a theological basis. When profits are a prime concern, using up the environment seems relatively unimportant. Another sees the environment as a trust under God to be carefully used. Others take an extreme view that turns nature into an object of worship. The theological implications of a work ethic, of the use of money, of political views—these are the kinds of things that divide people because opinions are held with deep feelings.

All of us face these kinds of conflicts at one time or another. We may be the accused or the accuser, but life's realities get to us. We may feel hurt or angry. Our self-image may suffer. We know genuine frustration because our best efforts have not been evaluated that way. How should we handle these events?

It helps if we view these conflicts as a natural part of life in a sinful world rather than as statements about our personal worth. Most solutions come by linguistic means; we have to talk about the conflict. Although it is hard for many people, talking is the surest way to correct misconceptions and promote understanding. It means bringing up the subject, not accusingly, but with the attitude of defining the problem: How do you perceive what is happening?

Confrontation is a learned art, and it takes skill.[4] Understanding, better relationships, and reconciliation are its goal. It is amazing how easily differences can be resolved and new levels of understanding achieved if people simply clear away the debris of some wrongly perceived notion. You hear people say, "That makes sense!"

A dramatic example of this occurs in the Old Testament. The people of Israel were incensed at the news that the Reubenites, the Gadites, and the half-tribe of Mannaseh, whose inheritance was on the far side of Jordan, had built a huge altar near the Jordan river, and they gathered at Shiloh to make war against them (Joshua 22:12). When Phinehas, the priest, and ten representatives from each of the tribes who had entered Canaan first went to inquire about how they could "break faith with the God of Israel . . . [and] turn away from the Lord and build . . . an altar in rebellion" (Joshua 22:16), they found they had misinterpreted the situation. Those on the far side of the Jordan had built an altar, not to offer sacrifices, but as a witness between them and the Lord, the God of Israel, that they were part of the children of Israel even though they had not crossed the Jordan, "for fear that some day your descendants might say to ours, 'What do you have to do with the LORD, the God of Israel'" (Joshua 22:24). Joshua records that the people of Israel essentially said, "That makes sense!" and blessed God and spoke no more of making war against them over this altar.

But not all conflicts dissolve with confrontation, even

when prayer precedes the encounter. Some differences come from low self-esteem. We are all an accumulation of our past and can stumble over things in our lives we have not worked out. Loving care-frontation offers the possibility of self-understanding if we are open to it, and usually it is self-understanding on both sides. Problems between people are often differences between expectation and performance, and sometimes "perceived" performance. We don't always have all the facts.

We have to be realistic, however. Some conflicts are too difficult to work out. We keep paying "top dollar" emotionally for some "irregular" relationships that could best be worked out elsewhere. It may mean a new job, a transfer, asking someone to resign, moving away, or avoiding certain subjects. It may also mean continuing to campaign for your point of view if you feel it is morally important. Some conflicts need the help of an objective third party who can point out truth that emotional involvement blurs. Conflicts cost something; we may pay a heavy emotional price to resolve them. They also offer the opportunity for growth. It is a risk one takes, and it is part of being human.

## Some Thoughts on Criticism

Criticism is a tricky business. To have no critical faculties is to be without discernment. To see only good means lying to yourself. On the other hand, we are prone to self-deception. You have heard this kind of assessment before:

I am firm; you are obstinate; he is pig-headed.

I share news; you carry tales; he's a gossip.

My child is independent; your child is willful; his child is a spoiled brat.

I tell it like it is; you are outspoken; he has no tact.

I have reconsidered; you have changed your mind; he has gone back on his word.

It slipped my mind for a moment; you are forgetful; he is senile.

I make a story interesting; you exaggerate; he lies.

I share my knowledge; you are long-winded; he is a bore.

I evaluate helpfully; you criticize; he nitpicks.

Criticism usually hurts; it touches us where we are vulnerable. What we call "constructive" criticism is hardly ever perceived that way. Most of us find criticism both hard to take and hard to give. We spend more time coping with our feelings than trying to understand and solve the problem. It does something to self-image and confidence. Someone did an unscientific survey to see whether women (the suspected victims) or men had the most difficulty accepting criticism; they found that it afflicts nearly everyone who is sensitive to other people, regardless of sex or status. Some give an appearance of gratitude for criticism but lick their wounds in private.

Here are some suggestions about criticism:

1. Do you have a right to speak? Not everything in another's life is your business.
2. Is your assumption accurate? Maybe there is something you don't know, another side to the story, some inaccurate perceptions.

3. Don't take the role of spokesman for another person or for a group of "theys." Fortifying your criticism with an invisible "cloud of witnesses" is downright damaging. "I'm not the only one who feels this way," or "a number of us feel . . ." If you bring in others, *name them*. Otherwise tell those people to take care of their own grievances. It clouds the relationships of the accused as he wonders, Who are all these people? It also limits the opportunity to clear anything up.

4. Be specific, not vague. Never say, "You always . . ." Make certain what you say is not a power play or that your poor feelings about yourself aren't being translated into criticism of someone else.

5. Watch your sense of timing in difficult confrontations. Don't use a "hit-and-run" tactic if you know anything about love.

6. Remember God is a God of justice. Both critic and criticized are known to him, and motivation is important to him.

Those who give criticism usually get it in return. That seems to be one of the laws of justice built into the universe. Criticism often attributes motives that are inaccurate and attack the person, not the problem. In contrast, "care-fronting" works on the problem. Criticism says, "You . . ." Care-fronting says "How can we . . . ?" Criticism usually creates negative vibes. Writers of critiques of art and literature usually feel it necessary to stand in a superior position and find something wrong. (Notice how most people fill in evaluation forms.) In its purest form, *criticize* means to consider the merits and demerits of, and judge accordingly. But its number two definition is to find fault openly, and that is the emotional flavor most people give it. The two meanings are far apart.

Evaluation is a less emotional word and safer ground. It is more objective and careful. We need to evaluate and discern. Expressing opinions may or may not be criticism, but people who don't like ideas are often intimidated by them. Criticism is often the *fear of difference*. Sameness is so much safer, less jarring. Consequently, the unusually gifted person is often criticized; a more average person is less so. The potential for growth is greater in the climate of difference, and we need to learn how to cope with it.

There is no good way to deal with the criticism that comes as a personal attack. However, you have to make certain that is what it is. Some people take every new idea as an affront to their person. Personalizing disagreement is a sure route to emotional collapse.

Personal attack uses a problem as a pretext for a message quite unrelated to the problem. The attack usually comes as a surprise and is highly emotional. The problem, which could easily be solved with open discussion, is magnified out of proportion. Essentially the attacker is saying, "I don't like you, and I don't like the way you do things." Forget the problem; it is the hostility that needs to be handled—*that* is the problem.

How to handle it depends on the relationship. What is the commitment? If this involves a husband and wife, they must hear each other and seek outside help if they cannot get to the root of the hostility. They have a covenant to keep. Whatever the relationship, the attack needs to be seen for what it is and then covered with love that forgives. Why does one person find it necessary to destroy another? The situation usually calls for a response of compassion rather than anger.

### 3. Troubled Marriages

Often our dreams do not match reality. People have expectations of a life together that comes out of storybooks. One young husband wrote to us on his honeymoon that although he didn't expect that his bride would be as stimulating a conversationalist as his favorite professor, he was surprised at how little there was to talk about. Since he rushed his bride into marriage during her sophomore year in university, we found the comparison ludicrous. How did it happen that he just found out now?

That might strike you as humorous, but people do seem surprised that being married doesn't automatically change the person they marry. In fact, a boaster seems to get tiresomely more boastful. Careless people end up marrying careful people. Early risers often marry people who stay up late. A quiet person is attracted to a lively talker, but the talker ends up wanting someone to talk with. Welcome to holy matrimony!

Conflict is inevitable when two people link their lives. Learning to resolve conflicts and communicate is the *work* of marriage. Couples have to learn to make something out of the raw materials they bring to their union. You can either make your differences the stuff out of which you forge something good—or give up. There is a price to pay to make a wedding into a real marriage.

Marriage troubles come from different sources. Sometimes trouble comes from being too close to family (no "leaving and cleaving," as some Bible versions phrase Genesis 2:24), and at other times the marriage lacks the support system that can come from family living nearby. Facing economic stress or illness with a small family on the far side of the country can be pretty lonely. And a loving, wiser, more experienced parent can give the perspective on your anxieties that your peers lack.

Competition between partners can lead to public putdown and disrespect in subtle ways. Hiding information to keep peace leads to a deceitful lifestyle and destroys trust. Verbal abuse is sometimes more destructive than physical abuse. The budget, the children, the household duties, television, and other equivalents become things to argue about. Conversation no longer builds; it destroys. In fact, the words hardly qualify as conversation.

Husband and wife can live politely together, avoiding conflict but each going separate ways until they drift apart. The substance leaks out slowly. Often a disappointment of some kind leads to deep introspection, and one shuts the other out. If a person is too busy to notice, distance can come quickly.

Whenever a child dies, a marriage faces a severe crisis. It is more than the loss of the child; it is the potential loss of their own relationship. The parents brood, and instead of comforting each other, they find reasons to blame each other. Statistics show that seventy-five percent of marriages that experience the death of a child end in divorce. Two people have trouble processing grief together unless they both come before God and share openly.

We have not yet begun to list the causes of marital problems, but it is sufficient to state the case. We are sinners in a sinful world. If a marriage lasts it is because two people decide to make it last. They are committed to the marriage even though they may not always like each other. No marriage ever succeeds because of the perfection of its partners, for marriage would then be obsolete. Marriage succeeds when two people want it to.

People are quick to speak of a destroyed love as if love

destroyed itself. Love is an active force, and we choose to love or not to love, to use this force or not to use it to cover each other's sins.

That may sound like preaching, but if yours is a rocky marriage at the moment, it is the bedrock on which to build. You may have to take a very uneven share of the building cost, but if you know how to trust God you have resources beyond yourself. The history of the world knows countless stories of people who made shaky marriages into good ones by the grace of God. In one marriage a woman may be giving one hundred percent to a twenty percent husband. It isn't fair, but she manages to create a climate that encourages both her husband and her children to be what they ought to be. Pain, misunderstanding, loneliness are hers, yes—but something very beautiful called *character* becomes hers, too, along with the peaceful fruit of righteousness. In another marriage, the husband carries the lion's share of building responsibility, and he does this because he made a commitment.

It does take two to make a relationship work, but if you are bent on even shares, you will probably quit in discouragement. The easy acceptance of divorce today allows a troubled person to sidestep solutions that might change them. Those who willingly stick by a commitment—covenant keepers, not self-actualizers—have a reward that goes beyond the pain of the relationship.

Help for marriage enrichment is available today through books and seminars as never before. No one is stuck with the smallness of his own solutions if he is open to counsel. Commit yourself to honest dialogue and learn from others *how* to communicate, but beware of emotional gimmicks that make things seem better without producing real change. Confession, forgiveness, renewed commitment to God and

His Word, fresh openness to hear each other and understand—these are the enriching elements that produce
growth. No easy formula exists that can be slapped on every
troubled relationship, but there are basic truths that can
open relational doors if they are tried.

   *Love (or charity) suffers long.* That is an important line from
Paul's great love poem in I Corinthians 13. Love is an
uncommon power that enables us before it demands
anything from us. Suffering itself takes no talent, writes Lewis
Smedes, but it is love that enables us to suffer long.

   Smedes says that to suffer is to be a victim. Long-suffering
is the power to be a creative victim. If love is the power to
suffer long, it follows that we ought to suffer long, but we
cannot mark dates on a calendar to measure out love's
power. Thus we are prone to ask, *How long, O Lord?* In general,
the answer is *very long—perhaps forever.* Or maybe just until
tomorrow. In any case, suffering long is not the same as
suffering endlessly.[5]

   Remember, your natural inclination is to cut suffering
short. Before you decide to stop suffering, make sure you
have not lost contact with God and his kind of love.

   "Love suffers some things longer than others. Marriage is a
special cause because marital long-suffering is done within a
covenant. No one can draw the line for others. God's kind of
love always moves us toward another person with no
demand for reward. This may be a rule of thumb: when I turn
off suffering for the sake of *my pleasure,* I turn it off too soon."[6]
Love suffers long so that healing and reconciliation may be
possible. Reconciliation is what love is all about.

   The emotional climate in our country encourages people
in troubled marriages to turn to divorce as the first option.
Instead it should be a reluctant last option. We don't know
much about suffering. We demand more from others, and we

put up with less. It keeps us immature, impatient, and shallow.

If you are even thinking divorce-thoughts at this point in your marriage, you need to look again at how God views covenants. Read Malachi 2:14–16 where God says he hates divorce and tells us why: "Because the LORD is acting as the witness between you and the wife of your youth." God cares about covenants, the vows, and promises we make in marriage. We talk about biblical grounds for divorce; God talks about covenant-keeping and reconciliation. He has not changed his mind about divorce. Jesus underscored this in his marriage statement in Matthew 19:9. His disciples, accustomed to the ease with which a man could put away his wife in their society, were sufficiently shocked to comment that if such is the case, it might be better not to marry. The bill of divorcement given by Moses, Jesus said, is necessary only because of the hardness of people's hearts.

The hypocrisy surrounding "biblical grounds" for divorce have made a mockery out of scriptural intent. Trying to determine who is innocent in a divorce can be a kind of game. The biblical grounds for divorce (to use the common phrase) is adultery. The Greek word is *porneia* (from which we get our word *pornography*), which covers a wide range of wrong sexual behavior. But moral innocence cannot focus simply on physical faithfulness. What of slander, an unloving spirit, a harsh attitude, lying, distrust—aren't each of these a kind of moral unfaithfulness, a ripping-off of another person that leads to marital breakdown? God's solution involves personal forgiveness, repentance, and reconciliation wherever possible—not a quick claim of "biblical grounds."

Whenever one person finds another annoying, it is easy to collect evidence to support the annoyance. It is like setting out to prove your conclusions are true—this is the opposite of love that covers a multitude of sins. Two people come at each other with "loaded guns." Discussions that could lead to the solution of differences run aground, and anger multiplies. A week apart from your spouse might give some perspective and provide the emotional space and rest needed to think straight. Such a vacation away from each other only works if people are committed to the resolution of problems. Taking a vacation is different from a trial separation. The latter almost always has a negative overtone that says, "We'll see if we can make it without each other." Don't be too quick to write *no hope* across a relationship. If God is God, then there is hope. It is important to act as if there is hope by following God's principles, which make it possible for him to work in your lives.

Rushing into marriage is not wise; rushing out of marriage is unwiser still. Hard questions must be asked when a marriage seems headed for failure: What is life for? What did our vows mean? Is this situation so terrible in God's sight that I have his permission to leave? Such situations do exist.

### 4. Divorce

Divorce is an awful sorrow, known only by those who have endured its devastation. It is more than smashed dreams; it is an assortment of emotions: rejection, failure, outrage, grief, guilt, and loneliness. It takes a long time to put one's inner life back together.

Whoever is left with the children suffers the added agony of helping them make sense out of life. The partner without the children faces another loss as do his parents. No matter how slick and cool people try to be over breaking a marriage, the tearing apart leaves scars on everyone. There is no good time to break a marriage. The more vulnerable you are—as a young mother, a person near retirement age, one with a lingering illness—the more outrageous it becomes. Over thirteen million children are being raised in single parent families, and the pain of those who have been left behind by divorce is unfair. They are the innocents.

Nevertheless this is the reality many face today. For every two weddings held in our country in the last decade somewhere one couple has divorced. Over a million children annually suffer through divorce. The divorce rate in the Christian community has zoomed ahead of the national average as the more conservative group follows the world's pattern. Yet this hasn't discouraged people about marriage. Many divorced people, lonely for the intimacy they once enjoyed, hurry into a second marriage without taking stock of why the first one failed. Blended families become a new source for tension: his kids, her kids, and resentment of new fathers or mothers. About fifty-seven percent of second marriages also fail.

Divorce is rightly called tragedy. Many people who did not even choose divorce are victims. It takes two to make a marriage work. When divorce occurs, it stops you in your tracks. But it is time to taken an inventory, not to look for a new relationship.

The first matter to take care of is your feeling of personal guilt. In Christ, failure is not final. What is your commitment to him? Have you asked God's forgiveness, spelling out what you know to be your personal failure and not just a vague grief? Are you asking him to show you more about yourself? When you deal with God you will find he lifts up bruised, broken people and restores them, teaches them, and guides them in the way. Your sorrow can be your biggest opportunity for growth and blessing. You will feel his presence in your life.

For this is what the high and lofty One says—
   he who lives forever, whose name is holy:
"I live in a high and holy place,
   but also with him who is contrite
   and lowly in spirit,
to revive the spirit of the lowly
   and to revive the heart of the contrite.

                                        (Isaiah 57:15)

That means dealing with feelings about your ex-partner. Until you do, God's grace can't flush clean your negative experience. It takes time. Some people try to fool themselves about "not caring," but peace comes only with forgiveness. When you forgive your ex, you will find it easier to forgive yourself.

Reconciliation must be an option as long as there is any hope. What does that mean? Only forgiveness can tell you whether reconciliation is possible. It may not be. Obviously, if your ex remarries or dies that option disappears. Many counselors agree that working through the trauma of divorce takes a minimum of two years. Deep wounds take time to heal, and it is safe to say that divorce may be harder in some cases than the death of a spouse. Don't be too hard on yourself if the old gremlins of fear, anxiety, and anger keep popping up. Dealing squarely with them is always the way to personal growth.

If reconciliation is no longer possible, then your options are to stay single or to remarry. But it is your relationship with God that is most important in either instance. Marrying out of strength, rather than weakness, is critical to your future. A weak, wounded, or insensitive person is not good marriage material, and to marry another who has not healed or dealt with self in deep ways is to court disaster. Lonely

people sometimes rush into a repeat of a previous relationship. Remarriage should not take place unless you have
genuinely tried to understand what went wrong, why it went
wrong, and why reconciliation failed.

On the other hand, having dealt with God and self, you
may find different satisfaction in the single life. Marriage is
not life's *summum bonum* or the panacea for all human hurts;
God is. Understanding that truth may be the biggest gain
from pain.

Getting on with life is important. God has new friendships
in store, new experiences, and a fresh sense of well-being for
you. He is the author of new beginnings.

## 5. Death

Death is final. It is a gaping-hole feeling, like being split in
two. Whatever the relationship that existed, it is no more.
Death exposes the fragile nature of life and makes us
vulnerable. It drives some to cling closer to God and find
their answers in his sovereignty; it drives others away from
God with angry questions of *why*? It is the great leveler; death
is no respecter of persons or age.

Suddenly relationships are past tense; you are no longer a
daughter or a son, a sister or a brother in the same way you
once were. Worse still, you are no longer a father or mother,
for the death of a child leaves terrible scars. But who can say
which pain is worse? To be fatherless or motherless confuses
and creates a pain deep inside that is hard to reach. And
what of the man or woman, young or old, who is so
intertwined in love with a mate, and then suddenly left
ragged and torn with grief?

Coping with death and its finality is exhausting; grief
makes a person fragile. One of our friends said she wished

she could wear mourning clothes so that everyone would understand that she was easily breakable and shouldn't be jostled.

Death surprises us, even when a person is terminally ill and death is a relief. We have to reconstruct life without that person in it, and yet we need to talk about the missing person, to be comforted by remembering, to feel the warmth that "belonging" brought. We need people who will talk with us and reminisce and not think our meanderings inappropriate or strange.

How well we do in the face of loss is determined most by our view of God. Believing in a sovereign God, a forgiving God, a merciful God, a loving God makes all the difference in our grieving. Surely, it eases the guilt that sometimes accompanies the finality of death and the words, "If only I had . . ." Those who hold God responsible for death's reality and turn their backs will have the hardest time. We will be happy again and that surprises us, and then we turn a corner, a memory flashes before us, and we are again filled with grief. Grief, said C. S. Lewis, is like a winding mountain path with surprising views and deep chasms.

Life needs rebuilding. We are still in the land of the living. Reality beckons. It is folly to destroy or neglect the good relationships we have while mourning the ones we have lost. A day may seem as long as a year, but even that passes. When death breaks a marriage, rebuilding is a lonely road. As in all other losses, though, it is not a road the believer takes alone. We find a resilience we didn't know we had; we survive. And God is faithful.

What can be said to widows and widowers, those who have lost their love? We are struck dumb as we write this, with our own grief and loss at the death of a young father so dear to us. It is compounded as we feel with his young widow and his three children—what do we say? Words seem empty. Yet after all the tears, we need a reminder to be thankful for what once was. A reminder of hope for the future—new grace, new satisfactions, more to life than we suspected. There are surprises along the way. Life goes on. God is still God.

But so many new things are frightening—things you didn't have to do before. Your loneliness can be exploited by others. You need wisdom you survived without before.

Death is another of life's events that stop us cold and make us listen. It is our opportunity to reassess our values, to line up our lives with new commitments to God, and to expect to meet him at every turn in the road.

### 6. Other Complexities

Life has other relational surprises that are frustrating. The people who want six children may get none, and the longings of the empty womb grow greater, rather than less, with the passing years. Those who want two may end up with six, even in this age of birth control, and coping with more children than income or energy is a frustration that tries their patience. They may say they weren't made to have that many children, but the evidence is to the contrary. They have them.

When we dream about our lives, our plans never include long-term illnesses where we can't take care of ourselves and be independent. Joni Eareckson never planned to be a quadriplegic. Think of her frustration at not being able to even dress herself.

Neither do our plans include wayward children who refuse God's love, flaunt our moral standards, and chase after false gods. Nor do we plan to pick up and go where we do not want to go, moving away from people we love and all that is familiar to us. Geographical dislocation is no small frustration to those who experience it.

A missionary friend once wrote to us: "We all need more grace to make us gracious. We need more grace to bear with the irksome things we think we see in others. We need more grace not to see them at all. And most of all, we need more grace to wear the unprovoked, lovely spirit of the Lord at all times."

Frustration in relationships takes many forms. Stress comes in many shapes and sizes. It is called *life*. And we are called as Christians to live with our eyes fixed upon a goal, seeking a prize not yet won, winning small battles along the way, knowing that the ultimate victory is assured by the One who called us to himself.

No one chooses frustration. Yet we find it along the way as a reminder that we were made for more than this. We often sing together a wonderful old hymn written by Adelaide Proctor (1825–1864) called "My God I Thank Thee Who Has Made the Earth so Bright." The last three stanzas seem especially meaningful in this context:

> I thank thee more that all our joy
>   is touched with pain,
> That shadows fall on brightest hours
>   that thorns remain,
> So that earth's bliss may be our guide
>   and not our chain.
>
> For Thou, who knowest, Lord, how soon
>   our weak heart clings
> Has given us joys, tender and true,
>   yet all with wings,
> So that we see, gleaming on high,
>   Diviner things.

I thank thee, Lord, that here our souls
    though amply blest,
Can never find, although we seek
    a perfect rest.
Nor ever shall, until they lean
    on Jesus' breast.

---

[1] Joyce Landorf, *Irregular People* (Waco, Tex.: Word Books, 1982).

[2] Betty Greene, *Summer of My German Soldier* (New York: Dial Press, 1973). Screenplay by Jane Howard Hammerstein, 1978.

[3] David Augsburger, *Caring Enough to Confront* (Ventura, Calif.: Regal Books, 1983), 11.

[4] We recommend *Caring Enough to Confront* and *The Freedom of Forgiveness* (Regal Books) by David Augsburger as excellent resources to help in the development of relational skills.

[5] Lewis Smedes, *Love Within Limits* (Grand Rapids: Wm. B. Eerdmans Publishing Co., 1978), 1–10. (Sentences taken from these pages are not necessarily in order.)

[6] Ibid., 6.

*chapter* 10

# What Love Can Do

*Love amazes us.* It is at once an abstract idea, an experience, a virtue, and an action. It is a noun; yet is has no personal meaning unless it is a verb. Love acts; it is not simply a sentiment. Love is of God.

Because we can know and experience love and set our wills to love, we have evidence that we are made in God's image. God loves. He is in loving relationship within himself; the Father loves the Son, and the Son loves the Father, and the Holy Spirit loves the Son. The Godhead is the perfection of love. God reaches out in love, creates a world, and peoples it with those who, bearing his image, can love him and one another. It is a *big* experience to be created with this potential.

If ever we need evidence of our fallen nature, we have only to look at our willful stinginess in loving others and God. Love is an enormously enabling power that has no limit because it comes from God. We never run out of love if we stay connected to its Source. "God has poured out his love into our hearts by the Holy Spirit" (Romans 5:5). Love is not a bootstrap operation, the result of self-effort. If love floods our lives, it is because God floods us with his love. We use his unlimited supply in our own limited ways.

Love is incredibly stretchy. It is the roomiest of all virtues; there is always room for one more person. Yet only God can love the world in a cosmic way; our love is limited to what we know. We fall into unreality at times by claiming to love the world and failing to love those closest to us. It is easier to declare love than to love.

Love is specific, not vague. And it is discerning. Love *knows* and understands. Love has a standard. Love is kind, but not all kindness is love. Love is not soft; it insists on what is right. Love hates whatever hurts people. It isn't love because we call it love. Love is not mushy idealism about the world and the people in it.

Truth is love's companion; it keeps love honest and from being swept away from reality. But love, in turn, softens truth. "Without love, truth's obsession with the facts distorts those facts," writes Lewis Smedes.[1] Love covers sin; yet love also exposes sin. Love is responsible. It has an abiding quality. It will never be transformed into something better, for it is itself the transforming power. Love begets love.

*What more can be said about love?* We use the word carelessly and use its power meagerly. Love makes relationships possible and makes relationships work. It makes them rich and satisfying. Love originates with God who loved and gave his Son as a sacrificial offering. Love chooses to live for others. It makes people givers rather than takers.

Love always drives us away from self and toward others. God's kind of love gives with no expectation of return. Love makes us givers who go the second mile, who forgive the past, who encourage new beginnings, who see and hear and care. That is love's power: It takes people seriously.

And because it takes people seriously, love listens, love builds other people. We say so much to another person about his worth by the way we listen. Each of us creates for someone else the climate for flowering or withering.

Eric Hoffer, the longshoreman-philosopher, became mysteriously blind for about eight years during his childhood. He tells of the Bavarian peasant woman who cared for him after his mother died: "And this woman, this Martha, took care of me. She was a big woman, with a small head. And this woman, this Martha, must have really loved me, because those eight years of blindness are in my mind a happy time. I remember a lot of talk and laughter. I must have talked a great deal, because Martha used to say again and again, 'You remember you said this, you remember you said that . . . ?' She remembered everything I said, and all my life I've had the feeling that what I think and what I say are worth remembering. She gave me that."[2]

Such a small thing this Martha did, yet what a large thing it became. That is the way of love. It is like a small seed capable of becoming a strong tree in the right environment.

Think of the children who *became* not philosophers or famous people or powerful magnates, but the best of who they were made to be because someone loved them and affirmed who they were. We have seen men blossom and *become* because of the love of a good woman, and we've watched women flower with creativity because of the affirmation of their mate. Troubled people find a straight path made by love; lonely people shine with the love wherewith they are loved. Love is the environment in which people grow best.

Love demands the investment of self. That is, it costs. It is like a gift we give someone. It costs energy; yet it is discreet and boasts not of its price or burden. Love serves others rather than obliging them. Love takes time. We never know what the smallest investment will produce in the years ahead.

As a boy Brooks Adams of the famous Adams family, made this entry in his diary: "Went fishing with my father—the most glorious day of my life." And so great was the influence of this one day's personal experience with his father that for thirty years thereafter he made references to it. Strangely enough, Brooks' father, Charles Francis Adams, one-time ambassador to Great Britain, made a different comment in his diary about the same day and incident. "Went fishing with my son. A day wasted."[3] Adults sometimes have a tragic blindness about what makes a wasted day. Love does not count the investment of time in a person wasteful.

*Love, in fact, is often extravagant.* Love is even sometimes foolish. Leo Buscaglia tells about the time his father came home and told the family he was bankrupt. He wept unashamedly in his despair. Mama said, "Papa, don't cry. We can make it," and all the children said, "Yes, don't cry; we will help." The next day Papa came home to find that Mama had prepared enough pasta dishes to make a banquet for the family. How could she do that? Didn't she realize they were bankrupt? Mama admitted she had sold some jewelry and said, "The time for joy is now while we are down. . . ." Extravagant love to lift the heart.

Mary did this for Jesus when she broke her alabaster jar with its costly ointment of pure nard and anointed the feet of Jesus (John 12:1–8). Judas complained about the waste, but the Lord Jesus received her act with gratitude. The Son of Man needed the encouragement of extravagant love.

Yet love is sensible; it pays the bills. It looks to the future, but it is never miserly or mean. It knows that there is time to smell the blossoms in the orchard and time to finish painting the room. Love stretches a casserole to include the discouraged neighbors next door. It takes the time to make a call at the nursing home and give an older person hope for tomorrow. Love is extravagant with hugs. Love touches people in many ways. Love knows it is not confined by dollars.

*Love has healing power.* It allows us to let go of the past and make new beginnings without settling all the old accounts. In love's presence details die. "Love's power does not make fussy historians," Lewis Smedes writes. "Love prefers to tuck all the loose ends of past rights and wrongs in the bosom of forgiveness."[4]

Our relationships—all of them, whatever they are—need this healing power with some regularity, for we are a fallen people. He who cannot forgive others destroys the bridge over which he himself must pass if he would reach heaven, George Herbert once wrote. And Jesus underscored this when he taught his disciples to pray. Forgiving and being forgiven are all of one piece. Love cannot be worn as a mask. If hate is there, it leaks out around the edges. Love cannot pretend. Genuine forgiveness is not easy. In fact, it may be the hardest thing human beings do. If one has to make an effort to forgive, the effort may be a sign of false forgiveness. True forgiveness is a liberation, not a burden. It frees both forgiver and forgiven.

But forgiveness is not overlooking sin or pretending about wrongs done. Love does not say, "Oh, forget it. It was nothing!" Forgetting it comes only after the forgiveness. Forgiveness costs. The one who forgives pays a price—the price of what he forgives. The guilty one goes free in forgiveness. Forgiveness demands a kind of substitution. The penalty is borne by the one who forgives. You may forgive the person who tries to ruin your reputation, for example, but you must bear the pain of his slanderous words. That is why it is so hard to really forgive. Only love can pay that cost— God's kind of love. God's forgiveness of us is the most costly thing of all: He gave his own Son who bore all of our sin. No wonder the Apostle Paul told believers, "Forgive as the Lord forgave you" (Colossians 3:13).

Love enables people to forgive—the "free gift" kind of love and forgiveness. Love enables us to accept people as they are—the people who hurt us, who oppose us, who fail us. Our love may be another person's only link to God. Give the gift regardless of the response. Feeling loved by God means sensing his love being poured into our hearts so that the overflow reaches someone else. Love's healing has reconciliation as its end. No one is ever too old for love, for no one ever outgrows the need for reconciliation.

Love sometimes gets angry, but it is wary of anger's pitfalls. Love's anger is not hostile or resentful but insists on righteousness. If anger has childish goals or lacks control, it is not love's anger. Love's anger avoids labeling people but labels sin instead. It desires another person's highest good and rejects anything that keeps the person from it.

*We do not always recognize love's ways.* Conflict sometimes seems a sign of the failure of love and discourages us. Instead it may be the beginning of the full work of love. Love must work to overcome the separation that exists between two distinct personalities. The great love is not the love that knows no conflict, but the love that weathers the storm. A love relationship is never static but is always changing and growing. Romantic love is not the whole of love. Only God's kind of love, which is always giving and accepting, is equal to the demands of a life lived together.

Love's opposites are pretty ugly and familiar—resentment, keeping score, malice, hostility, reliving the past, justifying our refusal to love, living for self. None of us likes these in others, but we often tolerate them in ourselves by giving them more comely names. They define all our relational hassles and eat like a canker inside of us. Our own insecurities and the smallness of our love may keep us prisoners of this ugliness. In contrast, we can let God's love flow through us like a refreshing, purging stream as the beginning of the freedom that needs to be worked out in our relationships.

In the end, love makes us servants of others. That is how most loving takes place. By its very nature, love obligates us, but it also enables us to do loving deeds and be loving people. "In the Kingdom of God, because the King is himself a servant, the title 'great' is reserved for those who, inspired by his example, spend themselves gladly and freely in the service of others."[5] Our model is Christ in loving action as he moves among human beings on planet Earth. He chose to love and we can also choose.

We won't all love evenly. Our human weaknesses will limit the flow of love in different ways, but love's power can work within our limits. Perfect love is an impossibility for imperfect people. Love is not a lofty ideal to admire from afar. You wade into it and get your feet wet. First you let God love you, and then you start loving others. Love begets love. God specializes in showing imperfect lovers more and more about love. We don't wait to be ideal people before we start loving. We are more like butterflies swooping high and then coasting low, sputtering over our loss of power in some situations while soaring strongly in others. And all the while God keeps pouring his love into our hearts by the Holy Spirit. It is more than enough for what we need.

Our relational problems—the mulish mate, the difficult child, the insensitive parent, the unfair boss, death, divorce, broken friendships, whatever—do not all suddenly disappear when we experience God's love and try to practice it. But love enables us to endure; it keeps alive our hopes of what could be; it it keeps us believing; it enables us even to suffer long. It prevents jealousy, boastfulness, arrogance and rudeness. It keeps us from being irritable or resentful. Love keeps us rejoicing in truth. Love carries all that is good; it holds life together. It carries a marriage, a friendship and whole families along. Love never ends, says the Apostle Paul in his great song about love. It is an eternal reality.

Beloved, let us love one another, for love is of God.

---

[1] Lewis Smedes, *Love Within Limits* (Grand Rapids: Wm. B. Eerdmans Publishing Co., 1978), 80.

[2] Calvin Tomkins, *Eric Hoffer: An American Odyssey* (New York: E.P. Dutton, 1968), 9–10.

[3] Reuel L. Howe, *Man's Need and God's Action, The Creative Years* (Greenwich, Conn.: Seabury Press, 1959), 23.

[4] Smedes, *Love Within Limits*, 7.

[5] R. V. Tasker, *Matthew, A Commentary* (London: Tyndale Press, 1961), 194.